79

$4.50

The ESSENTIAL POETS Series

Essential
Shakespeare

Selected and with an Introduction
by Ted Hughes

HarperCollins books may be purchased for educational,
business, or sales promotional use. For information,
please write: Special Markets Department, HarperCollins
Publishers, 10 East 53rd Street, New York, NY 10022.

Painting of William Shakespeare courtesy of the National
Portrait Gallery, London.

Designed by Nicola Ferguson

Printed on acid-free paper

Library of Congress Cataloging-in-Publication Data is
available upon request.

ISBN-10: 0-06-088795-8
ISBN-13: 978-0-06-088795-7

06 07 08 09 10 DIX/RRD 10 9 8 7 6 5 4 3 2 1

For Roy Davids

CONTENTS

FOREWORD

I HAVE ALWAYS BELIEVED that there is an untapped poetry audience, readers who are just waiting for the kiss of verse to awaken them into a landscape of emotion and image they've never experienced. Contrary to the common cliché, poetry is not actually difficult to understand, on at least one of the many levels a poem may work on—often just the simple, literary level of what the words are saying and what they invoke—"simple truth miscalled simplicity," wrote Shakespeare. Poetry has, and will always, play an important part in our lives. It's obvious to most that during the critical moments in our lives—that would include all rites of passage, from birth, through marriage, to tragedy and death— poetry surfaces to express our deepest feelings, elicits in us a wholeness and depth. A kind of shorthand of the emotions and the soul, a pure form of expression and experience.

So Ecco took it upon itself to go to the keepers of

the flame—they would be the most accomplished poets still living and practicing the art—to pick what is most essential from the canon that has been passed down to us. Thus began Ecco's ESSENTIAL POETS.

It's appropriate that we now celebrate our thirty-fifth anniversary with the reissue of this series, re-packaged but unscathed—a fresh format for the canon's ongoing journey into the hands and hearts of the new readers who will discover the magic in the distillation of this language they inherit. The music of the verbal object.

Daniel Halpern
Publisher
Ecco
An Imprint of HarperCollins*Publishers*

Essential Shakespeare

INTRODUCTION

IT HAS never been easy to settle Shakespeare into the succession of poets in English. According to most anthologies, he wrote only sonnets and songs. The reasons for this reluctance of anthologists to break into the sacred precincts of his drama and start looting portable chunks from the holy structures would make a curious chapter in the history of England's attitude toward its national hero.

Yet when the great speeches of his plays are taken out of context they are no more difficult to understand and appropriate than poems by other great poets. In many cases they are very much easier. It is no more difficult, for instance, to pick up, and make part of one's mental furnishings, the following:

> *To-morrow, and to-morrow, and to-morrow,*
> *Creeps in this petty pace from day to day,*
> *To the last syllable of recorded time;*
> *And all our yesterdays have lighted fools*

> *The way to dusty death. Out, out, brief candle!*
> *Life's but a walking shadow, a poor player*
> *That struts and frets his hour upon the stage,*
> *And then is heard no more; it is a tale*
> *Told by an idiot, full of sound and fury,*
> *Signifying nothing.*

than it is to come to terms with Yeats's "Death":

> *Nor dread nor hope attend*
> *A dying animal;*
> *A man awaits his end*
> *Dreading and hoping all;*
> *Many times he died,*
> *Many times rose again.*
> *A great man in his pride*
> *Confronting murderous men*
> *Casts derision upon*
> *Supersession of breath;*
> *He knows death to the bone—*
> *Man has created death.*

or with Eliot's:

> *Phlebas the Phoenician, a fortnight dead,*
> *Forgot the cry of gulls, and the deep sea swell*
> *And the profit and loss.*
>
>   *A current under sea*
> *Picked his bones in whispers. As he rose and fell*

> *He passed the stages of his age and youth*
> *Entering the whirlpool.*
>
> > *Gentile or Jew*
>
> *O you who turn the wheel and look to windward,*
> *Consider Phlebas, who was once handsome and tall*
> > *as you.*

In fact, if one specifies that "To-morrow, and to-morrow, and to-morrow" is spoken by Macbeth as he faces the leafy army that will put an end to his spellbound, murderous career (having just heard that his wife, who prompted the course of action that converted him from the king's loyal champion to a regicidal tyrant, has died), it actually limits the use of the passage for the readers. Its relevance is then confined to Macbeth's unique predicament in a sacrosanct, old-fashioned play rather than applied directly to our immediate plight as ephemeral creatures facing the abyss on a spinning ball of self-delusion. Obviously, by reading the passage out of context, one is missing the great imaginative experience of the drama—but one is missing that anyway. The speech on its own is something else, read in less than a minute, learned in less than five, still wonderful, and a pure bonus.

Accordingly, I have collected here a wide range of speeches from all the plays (except two or three) that seem to me self-sufficient outside their dramatic context and capable of striking up a life of their own in the general experience of the reader. In among these, I have distributed many of the sonnets and songs.

In a brief introduction to a selection of passages of the verse, it is best, perhaps, to stay clear of the metaphysical complexities of Shakespeare's great evolving mythos, from which the plays rise in a developing sequence. It is enough to keep in mind that this system, which is basically a psychic/religious conflict formulated in mythic terms, incorporates the violently deadlocked forces of the Reformation in England.* Throughout Shakespeare's fifty-two years, between the fanatic Catholic regime of Queen Mary, which ended seven years before his birth, and the Fundamentalist Puritan regime, imposed for a time thirty years after his death, England was making its subterranean somersault from one extreme to the other. During this period, Elizabeth I's Protestant police state enforced conformity with torture and execution. Her prolonged suppression of old Catholicism (the armies and armadas of the Catholic empire behind it) and new Puritanism (the *jihad* ferocity of the Continental Reformation behind it) was productive. The passion and paranoia of internationalized civil war were pushed down into the

* Ted Hughes, *Shakespeare and the Goddess of Complete Being* (New York: Farrar, Straus & Giroux, 1992).

private theater, the fiery crucible, behind every citizen's navel. The imagination of the era, so to speak, was primed.

In ways that are not difficult to recognize, the Elizabethan stage (the first two theaters were erected when Shakespeare was twelve) came into being as a safety valve, an externalization and self-psycho-analysis of this inquisitorial inner conflict. The clairvoyant depth of Shakespeare's involvement in the national trauma can be estimated from two of his dominant themes: the horrors of civil war, and the figure of the regicide who rules as a doomed tyrant. *Macbeth* has as much to say about the eventual emergence of Cromwell in the explosion of the Civil War, after Shakespeare's death, as *King Lear* has to say about the English King Charles—hunted like an animal through England by a ruthless commoner at the head of the English Army amid an apocalyptic "change of times and states."

Our understanding of how Shakespeare's imagination and his works actually came into existence and were able to develop as they did is limited—by two historical circumstances in particular. One of these is our strange ignorance of the intellectual and spiritual life of his milieu. The other concerns the complete loss of the Elizabethan acting tradition during the Puritan shutdown of the theaters from 1642 to 1660. The first of these was a crisis that is in one sense well enough understood. With Shakespeare's generation, the medieval world (the emotional world of his drama) came to an end and the Modern Age of Enlightenment (the pragmatic, scientific world of Sir Francis Bacon, Shakespeare's slightly older contemporary) emerged into being. The change was consolidated in the seventeenth century, when science, philosophy, religion, literature and general outlook took on the character, finally, of suppressive innovations. Though in many ways they evolved from earlier elements, they triumphed during what was, in one of its major aspects, a violent, revolutionary war. The shift from a society dominated by a religious struggle that had embroiled every citizen to one dominated by respect for scientific principles and a form of "reason" imposed by a social elite meant a thoroughgoing elimination, if not amputation, of all that had belonged to the fury and vital life of the religious struggle.

To understand the "fury," then, of Shakespeare's works, this lost world of religious war, internalized and expressed in dramatic fictions, has to be taken into account. That is not impossible. But what has evidently always been difficult is to understand how that world of embattled fanaticisms could produce such supreme inner illumination as is manifest in Shakespeare, in particular, and, in lesser and more fragmentary ways, in so many of his contemporaries. We cannot easily understand how it came about. The crucial facts seem to have disappeared.

The kind of sentence that was passed against the inner life, the imaginative life, of Shakespeare's world can be seen, to take one perhaps very relevant example, in the fate of the bizarre philosophy of Hermetic Occult Neoplatonism. This religious philosophy developed in Italy in the early fifteenth century in response to the deepening schism of the Reformation. It incorporated archaic mythic systems and various traditions of spiritual discipline, drawn from Pagan, Asiatic, Islamic, Gnostic, and Hebraic sources, into a giant synthesis centered on a Christ figure, and based on love of the Divine Source, in which Catholic and Protestant antagonisms were reconciled into a greater inclusive unity. This "lost" philosophy has been taken seriously and researched only in recent years, by Frances Yates. Mircea Eliade characterizes it as follows:

In a recent book, *Giordano Bruno and the Hermetic Tradition*, Frances Yates has brilliantly analysed the deep implications of the passionate interest in Hermeticism in this period. This interest discloses the Renaissance man's longing for a "primordial" revelation which could include not only Moses and Plato but also *Magia* and *Cabbala*, and, first and foremost, the mysterious religions of Egypt and Persia. It reveals also a profound dissatisfaction with medieval theology and the medieval conception of man and universe, a reaction against what we may call "provincial," that is, purely *Western* civilisation, and a longing for a universalistic, transhistorical, "mythical" religion. For almost two centuries Egypt and Hermeticism, that is, Egyptian magic and esotericism, obsessed innumerable theologians and philosophers—believers as well as sceptics and crypto-atheists.*

Bruno was in England between 1583 and 1586. His version of Hermetic Occult Neoplatonism was inseparable from certain memory systems developed from the mnemotechnics of medieval theologians. These systems are basically mental maps on which the whole *summa* of knowledge and speculation can be organized, anchored to "places" by visual mnemonic symbols, or emblems, or tokens, or, as Bruno also called them, "seals." The map was often some form of ladder between lowest Hell, through the worlds, to the Divine Source itself. The prototype was the Hebraic tree of Cabbala, where the entire universe can be arranged on the ten stations (Sephiroth) of the two Pillars of Justice and Mercy in such a way that the practitioner, in meditation, can climb, ideally, from the lowest to the highest. Thomas Aquinas authorized systems of this kind, partly through his own prodigious example, partly through his dispensation: "Man cannot understand

* Mircea Eliade, *Occultism, Witchcraft and Cultural Fashions: Essays in Comparative Religions* (Chicago: University of Chicago Press, 1976), p. 56.

without images." Frances Yates suggests that Dante's *Commedia* is virtually a memory map of Hell, Purgatory, and Paradise—and Dante's entire intellectual and spiritual world—organized by mnemonic figures, historic and mythic individuals set in places according to their spiritual significance, in a pattern that was by then almost a theological convention (where memory replaced libraries).

The combative Bruno developed and lectured and disputed on his own systems while living in England. Technically, his contribution was to fuse the tradition of memory systems with an Occult Neoplatonist vision, eventually producing what was virtually an occult mystery religion. The mnemonic images became the hieroglyphic language of a revelatory view of the material and spiritual creation. The images of his system were to be activated by magical means—by invocation and incantation, what might now be called elaborate procedures of self-hypnosis, but which he regarded as conjuration of elemental or demonic powers. He expounded this as a means of organizing the psyche and the knowable universe within an exalted vision of love. From his position, the dispute of the Reformation appeared (in his words) "like the squabbling of children." Before Bruno, the mapping of a "universal" memory had already been adapted to the form of a theater. After him, the English Rosicrucian Robert Fludd developed this concept even further, and there are strong suggestions that he modeled his Memory Theater on Shakespeare's Globe theater and made a link, of a kind, with Prospero by putting the magical activation of his system squarely under the figures of the great witches, Circe and Medea.

The occult aspect of the philosophy, as well as the limitless, computer-like power of thought and knowledge that it seemed to offer, held a potent fascination for Shakespeare's contemporaries. What it meant in practice was that the "sessions of sweet silent thought" of an Occult Neoplatonist became, ideally, a visionary trance in which he underwent some change of consciousness and attained access to the depths of his own mind along with a freedom of intuition, imaginative play, and sense of revelation normally impossible for him.

While still in England, Bruno adapted his seals to poetry, in a series of sonnets dedicated to Sir Philip Sydney. Sydney was already familiar with Occult Neoplatonism. His tutor had been John Dee, the most celebrated English mathematician and philosopher of the day, who became one of the most influential architects of Occult Neoplatonism's last phase. Since Shakespeare's patron, the Earl of Southampton, was the best friend of the Earl of Essex, who married Sydney's widow and inherited Sydney's social world, it is certain that Shakespeare was familiar with the ideas of both Bruno and Dee. And the aristocratic society behind *Love's Labour's Lost* (still Southampton's favorite comedy years after its first appearance) was certainly preoccupied with Occult

Neoplatonism, which at that time—circa 1593—was reaching the peak of its fashion in Elizabethan England.

For a while the reputation of this philosophy was high and its ambition boundless. Bruno, Dee, and other Neoplatonists traveled about Europe seeking a royal sponsor for this "loftiest and most imaginative idea of the Renaissance" that promised to resolve the Catholic/Protestant quarrel in a union of love. What it lacked, fatally, was any appeal to the masses. In its later phases, Occult Neoplatonism crystallized into various more or less secret societies and brotherhoods that were modeled on Islamic Dervish Orders and strongly colored by Sufi influences, as with the Masons and Rosicrucians. Frances Yates suggests that English acting groups were somehow involved in these orders. What is known is that Ben Jonson, satirizing occultism in general, brought English actors under his mockery in *The Alchemist* (produced the year after *The Tempest*), that Prospero is such an exemplary Occult Neoplatonist and magus that he is generally supposed to be a portrait of John Dee (when he is not supposed to be a portrait of Shakespeare himself), and that the main "sacred book" of European Rosicrucianism, *The Chymical Wedding of Christian Rosenkreutz* (published in 1616)—composed by a German author, Andreae, who had written plays "in imitation of the English dramatists" (his own words)—brought together many details that remind one of Shakespeare's last plays. What is curious is the completeness with which this hyper-imaginative, supercultivated world—which could well account for, say, Shakespeare's "romances," for his sophisticated and profoundly consistent use of the mythologies of the great religions, for his use of emblematic symbolism, both in his dramatic structure and his poetic style, and for his phenomenal abilities as an actively creative visionary—vanished.

Since Occult Neoplatonism openly challenged them both, Catholicism and Protestantism combined to liquidate it. For Catholicism it was devil worship and heresy (Bruno was burned at the stake in Rome in 1600). For Protestants, it was plain devil worship (John Dee was discredited for his conjurations of spirits and angels, and he died in poverty). For Puritans, it was devil worship and idolatry (hence memory systems, too, became anathema, even as an educational technique, in Puritan society). For materialist rational philosophy, it was superstition. For science, an absurdity. It disappeared from the intellectually respectable range of ideas and was pushed deep into hell (with the witches). In Shakespeare, or anywhere else, it ceased to be visible. Here and there it stirred in later centuries—in Goethe, to be wondered at, in Blake, to be deplored, and in Yeats, to be ridiculed. Only within the past fifty years has it begun to peep out again (though in general it meets with derision from the Puritan rationalist tradition). Only now does it become visible to such scholars as

Frances Yates. And only now can one begin to wonder again if there is more to Prospero than stage props.

This is only one aspect of the Elizabethan/Jacobean inner life that vanished and left no trace except in poetry. An incidental consequence of this cultural expurgation was that, soon after his death, Shakespeare became in some essential respects incomprehensible. The metaphysical system behind his drama, the religious or sacred aspect of his drama as the tragedy of Divine Love, became invisible. The extreme violence of his tragic characters is the fury of a very particular spiritual existence. But once that spiritual existence became unidentifiable, the fury came to seem simply "barbarous," merely violent in a secular way. Even the more intimate registers of his love-nature became inaudible. As late as 1766, a critic could confidently assert that if nothing of his works had survived but the sonnets, then he too would have been forgotten. Even Wordsworth regarded the final group, from number 127 onward, as "abominably harsh, obscure, worthless," and most of the rest as not much better. This sudden loss, in England, of the archaic, massive spiritual tradition that flowered in Shakespeare was accidentally confirmed—confirmed and made absolute—by the consequences of the Civil War, which coincidentally included that long closure of the theaters.

The convergence of factors that created a new literature at that point are a matter for a historian. But as far as drama was concerned, the decisive circumstance was that when the theaters reopened, the new mode was established by the half-French Charles II and his court, whose tastes, after fourteen years of exile, were French. The cultural abhorrence of everything that had preceded the execution of Charles I, and of everything that had characterized the England of Cromwell, made itself felt almost overnight, like an official censorship. The near-hysteria of this reaction can be seen in the paralyzed subjection of English poetry to the rhymed couplet for the next 130 years. More immediately, it showed itself in the attempts to translate those plays of Shakespeare's that could still be tolerated into the language "proper for a gentleman of culture and polite breeding."

In one sense, literary culture itself became a sort of prosthesis, implanted in the voice-box, that filtered everything through the thrice-distilled and decontaminated but traumatized sensibilities of the returned exiles, for whom the England of pre-1660 was, after all, a dangerous enemy country. In this way, that eighteen-year closure of the theaters became more than a break in rehearsals or the loss of two generations of continuity. It introduced a complete change of world. With the censorship that followed, it removed the last vestiges of the stage tradition within which Shakespeare's plays had been created. This might not seem to matter so much, in some respects. But it means that we cannot conceive what kind of electrical charge galvanized these huge structures into existence. We do not have the musical score — the tones and instrumentation, the pacing, the lift, the momentum that made *Antony and Cleopatra* actable any more than we know what kind of "music," what kind of power drive, fashioned the Athenian tragedies into such streamlined missiles of psychic force. If the Comédie Française tradition of performing Racine had been lost by a similar accident, no modern director could have guessed it back into existence.

SHAKESPEARE'S AUDIENCE made certain demands that no audience has repeated since. The basic problem for Shakespeare was that up to 1608, his audience — the famous Globe theater audience — was a microcosm of the whole English population. This audience was intact in the sense that in spite of the suppressed nightmare of their religious antagonisms, its members shared one passionate solidarity: They were part of a small, beleaguered garrison at war with the Catholic Empire. At the same time they comprised two distinct audiences. Along the upper edge sat the aristocracy, the intellectual nobility, in some ways as formidably educated and as exactingly cultured as Englishmen have ever been. And along the lower edge, in large numbers, were the common populace, the groundlings, many of whom could neither read nor write. This situation was greatly complicated, for Shakespeare, by the fact that both he and the theater were dependent—for their very survival—on both of these audiences, the most sophisticated and the most ignorant, the highest and the lowest, simultaneously.

His dependence on the Court and the Aristocracy was political. His dependence on the masses was financial. Throughout his career, the London City Authorities, dominated by a Puritan tendency, were trying to close the theaters. Shakespeare's livelihood—as part-theater owner, part-manager, part-producer, part-actor, part-playwright—must have seemed precarious. One can see why he kept up his Stratford wheeling and dealing in corn and malt on the side and lent his money out (at 10 percent) so briskly. Most years the theaters were closed for weeks or months by plague, and though the acting companies went touring during these periods, English towns were coming under the same strengthening Puritan outlook as London, and one by one (including Stratford itself in 1602) were shutting the companies out. The years in which Shakespeare attached himself to his patron, the Earl of Southampton, wrote his two long narrative poems, and began his great sonnet sequence addressed to the same lord were also the years when plague closed the theaters—mid-1592 through 1593 and into 1594. It must have seemed quite possible that playwrighting was over. Throughout this steadily increasing pressure of Puritan disapproval, the theaters depended absolutely on the favor of the play-loving court and nobility. With James I's accession in 1603, Shakespeare's company became the King's Men, performing regularly at court and even wearing the king's livery, so perhaps from this point their fortunes felt more secure—at least for the duration of the king's reign. But that only confirmed the fact that these courtiers were the most essential part of Shakespeare's audience. He made sure, therefore, that first and foremost his dramas gratified their tastes and supplied the intellectual satisfaction and amusement that they demanded.

As it happened, he was inclined of his own bent to give them what they wanted. The spiritual revolution of the age, which shaped their violent, exposed, and perilous lives, was exactly what preoccupied his imagination. But though the lords and the court controlled the legislation that kept the theaters open, and provided the audience for the scale and temper of imaginative drama that kept Shakespeare himself interested, obviously he needed the masses to make it pay. It is clear, from the way he dealt with it, that he recognized the problem. The playwright who rose to the demands of the nobility had to dive simultaneously to the demands of the groundlings. It was a dilemma that Ben Jonson, for instance, never solved.

What the playwright had to find, ideally, somehow, at every level—at the level of theme, of action, and of word—was a language of the common bond.

Shakespeare answered this triple demand as no other writer ever has. He devised a means of expression that communicated instantly with every level of his audience, but particularly with the two extremes. In other words, he found the common language of the highest and the lowest. It was also, in the end, the common language of a profoundly articulated, esoteric, spiritual vision and of a domestic, popular, tragic melodrama—which helps to explain why his plays continued to appeal to audiences that for one reason or another were blind to the vision. In solving these immediate problems, in what was almost a naively direct and practical way, he invented—as if incidentally, inadvertently—a new kind of drama and a new poetic vernacular.

It is easier to see how he found this language of the common bond if one looks at the kind of drama that shaped him before he shaped it. In the late 1580s, when he began to act and rewrite other men's plays, the ten-year-old Elizabethan theater was still wholly experimental. The stage tradition of the main bulk of the audience was made up of morality and miracle plays, and folk plays with the simplest puppet dialogue of the lowest common denominator. The first dramatists, university educated, idealized the classical Roman drama of Plautus and Seneca and were aware of the drama and, perhaps more important, the literature adaptable to drama, of Italy and France. The mixture was rich in suggestion, but it could not satisfy the peculiar English demand, that apparently infinite appetite to see the eruptive pressures of the late Elizabethan era molded into plays. Without controlling precedents, without oppressively revered earlier masterpieces, those dramatists had only the bare boards, the fever of global exploration, and that brand new, volcanic, terrible subject matter—the secret inner life, up to that point unexpressed, of the Elizabethan generation, which had to fight out, internally and psychologically, the War of the Reformation within a Protestant police state of nationalist loyalty.

The lightning flash that brought this theater to life was not Shakespeare but Christopher Marlowe. Two months older than Shakespeare, from slightly humbler origins but university educated (unlike Shakespeare, who left grammar school at age fifteen or earlier), he exploded onto the English stage in 1587 with *Tamburlaine*, Parts I and II. At a single stroke, he invented the drama for the new age. The astounding panache and brilliance of his spirit, and of his heroes—incarnations of a ruthless, limitless ambition—established a form. They established and made instantly fashionable a prototype drama that threw open Heaven and Hell and licensed all the ferocity of the Elizabethan dream. They also established a language. That volcanic inner life had found its authentic tongue. In the pitch and splendor of his lines, and the exalted, torrential yet compact eloquence of his long speeches, Marlowe caught the very flame that drove such meteoric over-reachers as Essex and Raleigh.

Marlowe was murdered—May 1593, age twenty-nine—before he could develop his discovery very far. But what he had created by instinct—and by a combination of terrific force and point-blank simplicity—was what one could call the carrier wave for a language of the common bond. Everybody, it seems, responded. What the whole audience wanted, evidently, from its highest to its lowest, with a kind of greed, was the language of more and more affecting and awesome emotions, more and more harrowing situations, more irresistible, stunning, hair-raising eloquence. It was addicted, one might say, to the for-tissimo eloquence of inner lives magnificently tor-tured. There have been many phases in the English theater, identified by various descriptive appella-tions, changing every few years. But never since 1608, when Shakespeare shifted his attention away from the audience of the Globe, have we had a the-ater characterized by that fullest possible verbaliza-tion of tragic frenzy.

We know how this appealed to Shakespeare. If it had not appealed to him so uniquely, if it had not provided the perfect medium for his peculiar artis-tic temperament, he would never have flourished so uniquely within it. Very early, in *Titus Andronicus,* he produced its most extreme and grotesque monu-ment. Perhaps Prince Hamlet speaks a little for

Shakespeare when, after reflecting on the necessary discretion and propriety of the actor's ideal delivery, he then calls for that speech which he "chiefly loved," a speech from a play that, as Hamlet says, was "caviare to the general," with "no matter in the phrase that might indict the author of affectation" but "an honest method, as wholesome as sweet, and by very much more handsome than fine." Yet his "chiefly loved" speech turns out to be that savage evocation of the infernal regicide Pyrrhus:

The rugged Pyrrhus, he, whose sable arms,
Black as his purpose, did the night resemble
When he lay couched in the ominous horse,
Hath now this dread and black complexion smear'd
With heraldry more dismal; head to foot
Now is he total gules; horridly trick'd
With blood of fathers, mothers, daughters, sons,
Bak'd and impasted with the parching streets,
That lend a tyrannous and damned light
To their vile murders: roasted in wrath and fire,
And thus o'er-sized with coagulate gore,
With eyes like carbuncles, the hellish Pyrrhus
Old grandsire Priam seeks....

and goes on to "mince" the Trojan King Priam with his sword while Hecuba runs screaming through the flames of the blazing city and the gods wail in heaven. Many modern tastes have found this speech excessive — to the point of burlesque. But though it leaves the actor blenched and trembling, it was not enough for Hamlet:

> *What would he do*
> *Had he the motive and the cue for passion*
> *That I have? He would drown the stage in tears*
> *And cleave the general ear with horrid speech,*
> *Make mad the guilty and appal the free,*
> *Confound the ignorant, and amaze indeed*
> *The very faculties of eyes and ears.*

However a post-Restoration sensibility might disapprove of it, this insatiable craving to break all barriers and enter a world in every way more impassioned and tremendous was a groundswell on which a judicious intelligence could float fabulous devices.

Or, to change the image, from the kind of power drive that Hamlet's words suggest here, one can imagine the momentum of delivery that lifted these great fuselages off the runway. One gets a whiff of what high-octane fuel they were designed for. And Hamlet's directions to the actors are to be understood as indicating the delicate controls of an immense airborne mass, a resonant containment of intensities that are beyond normal experience and therefore beyond normal means of utterance. In other words, the drama's essential common bond with the listener, no matter how intricate the verbal notation, must have been on the musical level of the physical and vocal orchestration, which was somehow internalized, perhaps in the way that can be heard when religious groups who maintain archaic tradition, or primitive groups, in performing liturgy, drama, song, or music, communicate with gods or imitate the voices and presence of gods. Some stage traditions have sophisticated this technique and humanized it without entirely losing that essential thing, for which García Lorca's image was the duende, and which is the very opposite of the extroverted, operatic, show-biz, noisy, loose, factitious commotion of performance that is generally interpreted as "passion" or "energy." The listeners simply happen to overhear, and find themselves transported, not because the eyes and ears are filled, but because the imagination is wrenched out of the head. Or the solar plexus, rather, is wrenched out of the body.

One of the least examined aspects of this kind of drama is the effect it must have had on its authors, especially those who, like Shakespeare, were harnessed to work-schedules of incessant production. The discipline must have amounted to a strange kind of psychic gymnasium. One has to imagine that constant effort to find the fullest and yet the most gripping and direct communication of the grandest themes, the truest realization and reliving of the most extreme human predicaments, on the greatest scale, to that broadest audience—and not in a study, but out there on the boards, in an electrified atmosphere of permissive (but serious) exploration. One remembers, too, that these early English dramas had an arterial link—not unlike the Greek tragedies—with religious rites that incorporated their primitive origins. They were still, in an almost literal sense, invocations with blood sacrifices—where blood was not the least important property. One has to wonder about the theurgic effect, extended over years, on the practitioner. When Shakespeare said, self-deprecatingly, in Sonnet 111:

> *almost . . . my nature is subdued*
> *To what it works in, like a dyer's hand.*

he was alluding not simply to his dubious, barely respectable trade as a man of the theater, but also to the psychological consequences of working and living in that tropical forcing house of optimal conditions and maximum demand. In this sense, these passages of Shakespeare's dramatic verse are the work of a professional in a way that no other verse is, in our whole tradition.

HAVING LOCATED the carrier-wave, Shakespeare still had to assimilate to it the great range of what he wanted to transmit. Unconsciously or no, he devised a kind of method. On the levels of both action and words, where it can be most easily observed, he followed the same kinds of procedures. These can be seen most easily in the way he assimilated his uniquely large vocabulary to his language of the common bond. Most of his 25,000 words (more than twice as many as Milton, his runner-up) had never been heard before by most of his audience. A great many of these words he used only once or perhaps twice — which is to say that they appeared as strange, and remained as strangers, remained virtually foreign words.

One question is, why did he do it, when most dramatists go in the opposite direction, simplifying their vocabulary and, like Racine, making do with comparatively few words in the interests of immediacy and as a short cut, too, to a common language? The more intriguing question is, *how* did he do it? How did he manage to introduce such a steady flow of strange words and yet reduce them to what turned out to be a massively successful language of the common bond? The first question has a historical answer. During Shakespeare's lifetime, particularly during his adult years, the English vocabulary expanded as never before or since. England as a whole seems to have been obsessed by eloquence, and particularly by the novelties of eloquence. Learned writers simply appropriated foreign words, particularly from the prestigious classical languages, and popular writers paraded them. A passion for the new words prevailed. The aristocracy brandished them as tokens of high status, were fascinated by skilled performers, and keenly appreciated any show of expertise. The middle classes imitated. The lower classes coveted. Word collecting clearly was a popular craze. On the evidence, nobody was more smitten by the craze than Shakespeare. And the whole range of his audience encouraged him in this. Their appetite for words, like their appetite for passionate scenes, could be relied upon.

The problem remained, however, whenever he used a new word: How was it to be understood? He could rely on the noblemen in the lord's gallery to give it instant meaning; they would simply translate it from the Greek or Latin. But what about the rest of the audience? The method he hit on, though eventually it produced an unprecedented and inimitable poetic dramatic language, had a kind of evolutionary history within his own work. It was also an ingenious systematization of what anybody does, automatically, when they come up with a word that an audience cannot understand.

Shakespeare's use of this method can be followed most conveniently through the development of a characteristic locution in which he balances two nouns or two adjectives on either side of an "and" and directs their combined and contrasted meanings to qualify a third word, always a noun:

To act her earthy and abhorred commands

is a famous example from *The Tempest,* written at the end of his career.

A beauty-waning and distressed widow

is an example from *Richard III,* twenty years before. His way of pairing the two qualifying terms, either side of an "and," like an aimed spear being balanced by the grip in the middle (like an image of his own name—"the Shake and speare of Will"), epitomized his use of his vocabulary, his structured use of a highly differentiated and composite vocabulary, and changed as his language changed. In other words, it changed quite violently at a certain point—which corresponds to *All's Well That Ends Well,* written around 1600, approximately the twentieth play out of the series of thirty-six.*

Eliot remarked that Shakespeare did the work of (at least) two separate poets. The first one simplified a language. The second one then developed it into increasingly subtle patterns of complexity. In fact, the process of simplification continued, but within the complexities. The first poet carried on, as laboratory assistant, simplifying and purifying the elements, while the second poet produced ever richer compounds. Eventually the simplification emerged again, or rather, at a certain very particular juncture—appearing first in *King Lear* and then

*With this play, his material underwent a revolutionary transformation. The "mythos," alluded to earlier, suddenly moved into his drama and became the substantial basis of the tragic sequence of plays which begins with *All's Well* and includes every subsequent play up to *The Tempest.*

consolidated in later plays, and corresponding to a radical evolutionary change in the mythos—the two processes melted into a strange new fluid substance, musically more delicate and intricately bonded than anything before it, dramatically more simple and direct.

Throughout these transformations, that aimed and balanced lance of a phrase makes its way, reflecting the shifts. Up to *All's Well*, it played an active role, but without special duties. Through the earlier works, the vocabulary, though quite large, is not adventurous, and in the example given above from *Richard III*, the novelty of "beauty-waning" is a novelty of combination, not of actual vocabulary. Even there, though, the interplay of the two qualifiers seems deliberate and nicely judged: "A beauty-waning and distressed widow" presents the widow from two points of view—the objective, "beauty-waning," and the subjective, "distressed." The effect is to make a small scene, where the outer widow, on one side of the stage, is looking at the inner widow on the other side. The "and" becomes the electrified space between and the lifted square of the stage. Both figures are fixed in a somewhat hieratic pose, strongly lit. How far this effect depends on that "and" can be seen if one removes it. "Beauty-waning, distressed widow" is a crumpled heap: "beauty-waning" has become self-conscious, she seems overdressed, and the tension of drama has evaporated.

Another example from the same play shows the

same scenemaking function even more clearly. The king is speaking:

> *Be judged by subject and inferior breath.*

In a straightforward sense, "subject" and "inferior" are the king's view of the outside and inside of the breather—what ought to be his formal, servile relationship to the king, and what ought to be his inner, slavish reality. But the opening phrase, "Be judged by," having already introduced the idea of the "breather" as the king's judge, suspends over the word "subject" the idea of "lord and master" and over the word "inferior" the idea of "superior." The first half of the equation now presents an inversion of social hierarchy, the second an inversion of psychological values. Without being complicated or obscure—being in fact fairly obvious and open—the line has nevertheless become a mini-projection of a key Shakespearean scene, the king confronting the victorious rebel.

Twelfth Night was possibly written within the year preceding *All's Well*. In this play, that first simplifying poet achieved his ultimate refinement of limpid, flexible, direct, warm simplicity, establishing a pentameter norm that has stood poetry in English in good stead ever since. But the very opening speech, the famous:

> *If music be the food of love, play on,*

ends with a slight lexicographical flourish:

> *O spirit of love! how quick and fresh art thou,*
> *That, notwithstanding thy capacity*
> *Receiveth as the sea, nought enters there,*
> *Of what validity and pitch soe'er,*
> *But falls into abatement and low price,*
> *Even in a minute.*

The three words here that might have given his groundlings pause are "capacity," "validity," and "abatement." On the other hand, they were all words that some other Shakespearean character might have pounced on, fondled and turned: "Fine word, capacity!" (as several here and there are inclined to do). And they are all words that would be appreciated by that higher audience, the classically educated phrase-collecting lords.*

The striking thing is what Shakespeare does with each of these words. "Capacity" is immediately reduced to a plain image: "Receiveth as the sea." In other words, it is translated: capacity = spaciousness, roominess, infinite ability to contain. In a similar

---

* There exists at least one record of "fine phrases" culled from a Shakespeare play, scribbled during a performance, or shortly afterwards, with errors, from *Henry IV, Part I*, on the blank pages of a notebook otherwise filled by notes of a lecture by Harriot, the mathematician and friend of Raleigh.

way, "validity," which was probably a new word to most, previously used only in law, is translated by "pitch," a common word meaning "height," or "calibrated position on a scale." "Validity" becomes, instantly, "place on a scale of values." He deals with "abatement" even more plainly. While he tosses the fine word to the lords' box, he bends to the groundlings, and quite shamelessly adds "that means—low price."

None of these are full-blown specimens of his device where the two balanced words qualify a third, but all demonstrate a reflex which at this point in his work is developing, as if with careful thought, into a system where the new, unfamiliar word from the "high" language is balanced, interpreted, and *translated* by an old word (or words, or image made up of old words) from the "low." In practice, this usually becomes a combination of one word of classical derivation with another word of native (old English, Celtic, or Norse) derivation. Faced with what were virtually two languages, made more distinctly and urgently so by the presence of the two audiences, Shakespeare rose to the occasion (some of his colleagues, such as Nashe, were aware of the "double language" problem, but none systematized a solution as he did) by speaking both—the full foreign text and the full translation—simultaneously. He was pushed to this, one might say, by his perverse insistence on using such a huge number of the new words—by his determination, one might say, to provide a unique gratification to the addicted nobility, a shower of thrills to everybody else, and one supposes no small satisfaction to himself.

This masterful democratization of high language and low had an accidental cause, as I have described, but it bears some sign too of a deliberate motive. That "deliberate motive," one can imagine, lay in Shakespeare's idea of welding his audience into a single thing. This would be of a piece with what emerges, ultimately, as the overall ethical concern of his drama: his search for an imaginative synthesis of archaic religious emotion and new, moralizing, idealistic, suppressive reason, of the painfully colliding old world and the new, in a harmonic pattern of containment for all religious, cultural, and social extremes. At bottom, it was a heroic attempt to resolve, in language, the layered, fissile antagonisms within a nation formed by successive, brutal military occupations of which (as such plays as *Cymbeline* show) he was exceedingly conscious. Roman had invaded and suppressed Celt, creating — for 400 years — a double nation. What survived was then invaded and suppressed by Anglo-Saxon. Anglo-Saxon was invaded and to a large degree suppressed by Norse. What emerged from that was finally invaded, and brutally suppressed, by the Norman French. At each stage, the inner sense of a double nation — where a native, autochthonous breed of indigenes, speaking an old language, with old local emotional allegiances, was ruled over and oppressed by people of a foreign stock, speaking a distinctly different language, with allegiances to the continent—rearranged itself and deepened. Shakespeare's enforced intermarriage of the racial strains within his poetic style was in this sense a political and social act without precedent. And after his death—when the divisive process was repeated and the Restoration imposed, as I mentioned earlier, a culture hostile to old English but loyal to French values—the high language and low language did not merely fall apart, they were forcibly separated. Shakespeare's hybridization and crossbreeding, for all its superior vigor, multiple genetic resource, and incidental, exotic, half-caste beauty, became a barbarous offense against gentility.

The *accidental* poetic result, which in some ways is the most curious and intriguing aspect of Shakespeare's invention, is in part obvious, in part enigmatic. The obvious elements lie in the suddenly focused activity of contrast and comparison between the two halves of the "translation," which in turn is partly an explosive burst of analysis, partly an explosive burst of metaphorical suggestion. This becomes even more evident in later examples. The shaping and shading of deliberate art are, perhaps, what each example presents uppermost. Shakespeare's miraculous ear for molding a phrase, and his inspired eye for the hieroglyphic or composite symbol, clearly from the very first hint grasped the bewitching possibilities of his novel verbal combination, and of his double device in particular. I called this device lance-like, but he seems to have modeled it almost on the pattern of a coat of arms: two families of meaning, two ancient etymological lineages, each condensed to a rich sign or crest or sigil, impaled on a heraldic escutcheon. From the earliest examples, as in "A beauty-waning and distressed widow," he is aware of the iconic, ennobling effect of the balanced form, the moment of grandeur, the lift into solemnity and distinction out of the colloquial helter-skelter, the sudden deepening of perspective. The result, even here, is enough of a self-contained circuit, internally active enough, to be a kind of mini-poem in its own right.

This sense of shaped beauty, radiating from what is also, usually, an emergency makeshift of translation, is worth looking at more closely. It becomes more pronounced, suddenly, when that second poet, the complicator, enters with *All's Well That Ends Well*. In this play, the complexities of all Shakespeare's procedures take a quantum leap. Accordingly, the autonomy and almost organic wholeness of his verbal device become hyperactive, crystallizing a process that transforms his vocabulary, yoking disparate worlds of reference and opposed metaphysical realms violently together within the new language of the common bond.

A single speech will illustrate this changed character of the language and the suddenly new special duties that the device now performs. To make full sense of the passage, one needs to remember that

the plot of this play concerns the total and uncondi-
tional love of the orphan Helena for the young
Count Bertram, with whom she has grown up. Igno-
rant of her love, Bertram goes off to the court. The
French king is dying of an incurable fistula. As it
happens, Helena's father, a great doctor, bequeathed
to her the cure for this specific malady. With a mo-
tive, she follows Bertram to the court and makes a
wager with the king—that if she cures him he will
give her the husband of her choice. The king cured,
she chooses Bertram, who is compelled to obey the
king, albeit outraged, and immediately abandons
this new wife, fleeing to the wars in Tuscany in the
company of the worthless swaggerer Parolles. The
rest of the play concerns the punishment and
correction of Bertram, who in seducing an Italian
woman is tricked into impregnating Helena, and fi-
nally humbled into accepting her as his true wife.

Before the action has developed, the dying king
welcomes Bertram to the court, remembering his
old friend Bertram's father with the words:

Me-thinks I hear him now; his plausive words
He scattered not in ears, but grafted them
To grow there and to bear—"let me not live"—
Thus his good melancholy oft began,
On the catastrophe and heel of pastime,
When it was out—"let me not live," quoth he
"After my flame lacks oil, to be the snuff
Of younger spirits, whose apprehensive senses

All but new things disdain, whose judgements are
Mere fathers of their garments; whose constancies
Expire before their fashions. "

The language of this passage typifies the new complexity, moving tortuously from image to image. In one sense, the density is a busyness of "translation." But out of the thick of it flashes the mysterious line "On the catastrophe and heel of pastime," bringing one to a halt.

Shakespeare's love for new words we take for granted, but to assemble and deploy the extraordinary number that he did suggests a peculiar diligence of method. One supposes he had some special magnetism, and words just stuck to him, instantly organized and aligned like iron filings in a magnetic field. But he himself remarked that a new word has to be "looked upon and learned." If other evidence is valid and he used a Brunoesque mnemonic system, then it is likely—whether or not he actually set it down in the "tables," or notebook, that he mentions here and there—that he fixed each new word not only with its general translation but with an image as well, a hieroglyphic "token."

In its context in the line, "catastrophe" is almost bizarre. Combined in this way with "pastime" it is either mismatched or—perhaps—explosive. Why should Shakespeare need such a violent irruption of suggestion at this point? Maybe its raw oddity betrays the uncertainty of experiment. In this sense, the line is typical of the intermittent, jerky vehemence of the verbal complexities of *All's Well*. It would rip the fabric of any earlier play. At the same time, it undeniably works. One goes back to it, and finds it livelier than ever.

By regarding the line as a slightly modified "new word" entry in his "tables," where the word to be mastered is matched with its translation and fixed with its mnemonic image, one sees not only how "catastrophe" is the perfect and even the inspired word for the occasion, but how the whole line now illuminates the play itself—and from several different angles. Shakespeare knew "catastrophe" in its precise meaning as the sudden change, the "turn" which produces the closing event—generally disastrous—in classical drama, though it already carried, as a learned, literary word, the general meaning of "final scene," "last and lowest point." Somewhere in his imagination, as if in that mnemonic note, he had made the association of "catastrophe" as "last and lowest point" with the homely image "heel." Since this is incomplete, he had then enriched the plain heel with the supplementary idea of the calamitous end of a Greek tragedy, coming up with "Achilles' heel"—a typical piece of wit. Having got that far, since Achilles was the champion athlete of the Greek host, the mighty runner, this Achilles' heel automatically associated itself with the idea of sport or strenuous "pastime." All this now emerges from the line as the king speaks.

As they are spoken, the words direct the listener's attention beyond the line, into the scene, and into the play behind the scene. At once, "catastrophe and heel of pastime" ceases to be bizarre. The speaker confronts the end of his life, which is being brought to a premature, calamitous close by a fatal disease. And listening to him is the young Bertram who is about to throw away his "soul." Accordingly, in this phrase the idea of "pastime" (the pleasant, unforced, amusing sport that displaces what might otherwise be boredom) becomes a drama with a tragic end—without ceasing to be idle play. "Pastime," that is, has become a metaphor for the life which is let go by, foolishly and idly, because the owner cannot waken up to the fact that it is his serious role, his only opportunity to perform and live, until it is on the point of ending. Then, too late, he grasps that it has been, because he wasted it in error, a tragedy, and that the end is therefore a "catastrophe." In this line, seeming to refer in courtly periphrasis to Bertram's father, the king speaks directly and painfully of himself, and directly and painfully of Bertram as well, making an image of what—if it were not for Helena's healing power and redemptive love—would be the action of the whole play.

Having united these two potentially tragic fates in his new word, Shakespeare immediately translates it. While his high audience relishes the sinister implications of "catastrophe...of pastime," he explains it to his lower audience as if saying, "In other words,

heel of pastime," which carries just enough of a hint that "the end and lowest point" of pastime has in this case wrenched or bruised itself. Finally, to be absolutely sure that the lowest groundling understands it, he adds that almost lamely plain explanatory phrase: "When it was out," (i.e., when the pastime was over). But already one can see that Shakespeare is doing far more than simply glossing "catastrophe." His little translation machine has become—accidentally, coincidentally—a factory of riddling metaphors.

"On the catastrophe and heel of pastime" is remarkable, first and foremost, for its lack of syntactic controls. Every possibility of relationship, between the three elements, is not only left wide open, but all are simultaneously energized. One is forced to ask exactly what "catastrophe" and "heel" mean in this oddly empty yet teeming context. Their physical position alone—both being lowest and rearmost—is all they seem to have in common. Yet this is control enough; it makes the two words synonymous enough, for the spark of likeness to leap—which is the life of the gadget. That spark sets these two otherwise utterly freed and unrelated worlds of reference spinning around "pastime" like electrons around a nucleus. Each is suddenly alive with all the properties of the others, liberated and galvanized into inexhaustible, figurative new life. And every possible relationship presents itself as a riddle. How is a catastrophe like a heel which is like a pastime?

How is a pastime like a heel which is like a catastrophe? But first of all, how is a catastrophe like a heel, simply? The suggestive power of these ideas is explosive—as if heel, that fundamental part of the self, could experience a nightmare, and like some kind of aerial receive and transmit all the tragedies possible to man. Simultaneously, the crowded, howling universal concept of catastrophe orbits there, in surreal form, as a human heel. But the "heel of pastime" is more particular.

The Achilles' heel is proverbially a strong man's weak spot. The Achilles' tendon was the only point at which death could take hold of the great hero, being the part that his mother, Thetis, nipped between her finger and thumb when she dipped him into the immortalizing Styx and which therefore remained dry, vulnerable, and mortal. In general, damage to this mainspring of the body is the most disabling of athletes' injuries. Moreover, the Achilles' tendon carries in itself a primal fear, being the "hamstring" slashed by hunters and predators from the beginning of time.

Achilles was a sacred king (like the speaker) and died when a poisoned arrow pierced his heel—as the speaker is dying of the toxins of a *fistula,* which is "a long, narrow, suppurating canal of morbid origin," like the wound of a poisoned arrow. In this way, the "catastrophic heel" and the "heel of pastime" return to the king's own sickness, which corresponds in the plot to Bertram's moral blindness, making a

double image of the inmost theme of the play. The line has now become a crystal of the entire play, faceted for different angles of inspection, revealing different but coexistent and interdependent worlds.

A similar process, in only slightly looser weave, continues throughout the king's speech. At each step of the argument, a novel concept is introduced, usually with a not altogether familiar word, and then, in familiar words, translated into a familiar (hieroglyphic, mnemonic) image, simultaneously creating a total and self-enclosed scene. In the second line of the king's speech the uneasy "plausive" was a new word. *The Oxford English Dictionary* gives precedence for the first recorded use of this adjective to the dramatist Heywood, in 1600, but even if *All's Well* did not precede that (and we are not sure), it was a word that, for Shakespeare's purpose, needed translation, which he gives by rich implication in the next line and a half in a single image that could not be misunderstood. At the same time, this image creates a world in which wise, praiseworthy words, deliberately planted (even, perhaps, a little against the listener's will), eventually bless the listener— which is what the king is actually doing here—planting in Bertram's ears an unwelcome homily about headstrong, selfish youth, which he will, at a point in the future, suddenly understand. And that, in turn, presents an image of the play as a parable of the prodigal son's belated awakening.

After the concentrated detonation of effects in

"catastrophe and heel of pastime," the king moves on to a series of metaphors, each of which translates a difficult, manifold concept into a plain image. To begin with, the speaker wishes to say that he does not want to live after his youthful vigor, burning out, leaves him world-weary, to depress and discourage younger spirits with obsolete, unseasonable admonishments. He translates that instantly to the clear, concise, familiar image of the oil lamp, where each word is likewise simple and familiar. Simultaneously he creates a scene—the old, used-up person as a burned-out blockage between the flame of living and the oil of vigorous new life, which is again an image of the play, where the sick king is himself an image of the false self of Bertram—the Bertram who rejects Helena's love and prefers folly. Both the king and Bertram are the "snuff." When the king is healed and Bertram's offending self is whipped out of him, the snuff will have been removed—and new oil will flow to the flame in new life. In the next line, the judgment of young men is good for nothing but to sire not new selves (the theme of the play is the search for, and the finding of, that new self for both the king and Bertram), but merely the latest garments in fashion (Bertram is being led astray by Parolles, a "jackanapes with scarfs" whose "soul is in his clothes," a creature of empty words and outward show, a doppelganger who will be stripped naked finally). The constancies of young men are a form of

mental garment (like Bertram's love-vows to Diana, whom he will instantly abandon after he has, as he believes, seduced and impregnated her) that cannot live as long as the fleeting fashion in which they dress their bodies.

This magnesium, pulsing glow of a constant metaphorical enthrallment, a continuous play of riddle, a constant simultaneity of at least two worlds, characterizes the new language that arrives with the second Shakespeare, the complicator, in *All's Well That Ends Well.* From the beginning of his career, his illustrative images tend to be images of some prominent theme of the whole play. But now these images arrive not at leisurely intervals, but as a tightly interconnected hieroglyphic text, a continuum of signs parallel to but separate from the immediate meaning of the speech, and referring back into the body of the play, holding the whole crowded, heavily loaded aircraft reverberatingly present behind whoever happens to be at the controls. The effect is to give each line, each phrase, even each word the dimensions of the entire play. The play itself is thinking, in these lines of the king's speech, defining itself, turning itself this way and that, searching among all possible images for new images of itself, and trying them on. As the voice touches each successive image, the whole story lights up. Phrase by phrase, the king's voice moves through a flickering succession of holograms of the entire play. At the same time, confronting Bertram, he is saying clearly and directly what has to be said.*

In responding to the need for a language of the common bond, Shakespeare has invented, as if accidentally, an extraordinary new form of English. He democratized high language and low with what amounts to a forced system of intermarriage that goes right through his usage. This invention reflects his interfertilization of high seriousness and low comedy on the plane of action. In the subsequent dramas— *Troilus and Cressida, Measure for Measure,* and thereafter—he welded the contrasts and conflicting extremes of his new material simultaneously, on the planes of action, theme, and words, into this composite, dramatic language—the new, total complex of his expressive means which was at the same time a new universe of referential possibilities for his inventions and a "language of the common bond." And the strange fact is that while accomplishing all this, for that very specific and historically brief situation within the theater, he invented a language that is somehow closer to the vital, expressive life of English, still, than anything set down since. The harder one looks at it the odder this seems. The inner complexity and precision of, for instance, the king's speech above, which reproduces in itself

* However satisfying as a "poem" the speech out of context may be, this is the argument for not resting content with it as it stands alone.

the stresses and tensile structure of the whole play, like that of a great flying machine, as if it were a sort of fractal of the whole play, it seems also, somehow, homemade, improvised. It has a ramshackle air, like a prodigiously virtuoso pidgin. This is simply characteristic of his mature style. The proverbial durability, that immovable, engraved monumentality of his phrasing, is countersunk in syllables that are full of imps and goblins. His images have the sacred quality of icons, but they are also juju dolls. His masterful formulations smoke with chaos. Inside his noble Othello, his royal Lear, his proud Coriolanus, are Caliban, the Fool, and even Aaron the Moor. It should tell us something, presumably, that his towering oeuvre opens with Aaron the Moor and ends with Caliban, the son of an African witch. Those figures correspond, in the psychological substance of the plays, to the insuppressible, aboriginal dialect spirit in his language of the common bond, the insubordinate, wild root of his mother tongue, which in turn corresponds to the unkillable demon of subjectivity, of what is inborn and primal.

Shakespeare's imperious conscripting of Latinisms always strips off their togas and juggles irreverently with their noble parts—not quite as malapropisms but always in the all-licensed spirit of dialect. Regularly this takes the form of a literal and almost concrete use of the abstract Latinate word in its root meanings. A typical example would be Queen Gertrude's:

Alas, how is't with you,
That you do bend your eyes on vacancy,
And with the incorporal air do hold discourse?

as Hamlet, his hair on end, speaks to the empty air that nevertheless holds the body—that should be the corpse—of King Hamlet in the shape of the Ghost and which—Shakespeare cannot have missed it—is "oral" and speaks back. One does not suppose that Shakespeare gleefully thought this out, like a crossword clue; he drew naturally on the dialect instinct to reduce "incorporal" to "what has a corpse in it" and, as a bonus, one that speaks. In other words, the Latinism has been dismantled, in an almost comic way, to solid and familiar things which at the same time vitalize the abstraction with action and world.

This is pure dialect technique for naturalizing (resurrecting) the words of strange (dead) languages. A more willful form of it mis-hears the current and root meaning of the Latinate word to lip-read more familiar and vital words into its syllables. This device differs from the sophisticated speaker's punning (which is a slightly guilty escape into the liberty of dialect and, because guilty, can hardly be indulged except as a joke, which feels obliged to apologize for itself) in that it is serious, unself-conscious, and generally part of the emergency mobilization of every resource conducted in an effort not merely to give the whole picture but to reproduce the whole event. A popular example of this is the notorious "aggravate." No cultivated speaker would use the word in its vulgar sense of "to goad beyond endurance" (which is a sharp indicator of just how rigidly English "high" language still is in its post-Restoration phase: the word would be rejected in post-Restoration terms). Yet it is more than a Joycean vintage blend of "irritate, anger, aggrieve, exaggerate." It releases the deeper, old English physical core complex of "growl, gripe, grate," and from beyond that again, deeper still, the echoic, universal, animal "gr"—the molar-grinding groan of the biter about to bite what has bitten it. The word inherits a much more powerful meaning, and a far more expressive life, by this wrenching misuse in "dialect" than its precise Latin sense can ever carry. Yet the precise sense has not been displaced altogether. The new sense, which includes something of the precise sense, has been added to it. Shakespeare is doing this, just slightly, constantly.

But much more elaborate games are going on too, all part of the same irregular, opportunistic, dialect playfulness. In *Cymboline*, the riddling prophecy of the denouement is deciphered by the soothsayer, who glosses the cryptic, mystifying phrase, "a piece of tender air" as "mollis" (Latin: tender, soft) plus "air" (English: air) = "mulier" (Latin) = "wife." The high-handed drollery of this etymology suggests just what (very like the submerged, parallel, absurd imagery of a mnemonic system or the ubiquitous whisper of Lear's fool) is supplying some of the skewed, parabolic spin, not just to Shakespeare's Latinisms but to his terms in general. It is the visible, turbulent wealth of his truth to himself, his total, inclusive acceptance of all the battling (dramatic) contradictions within his own subjectivity. The effect is always to re-create everything he touches out of his own blood-hot psychic substance and to suspend the rather massively molded finality of each line's verbal physique over a gulf of inner apprehension and nervous self-awareness—more revelatory of emergency in the body's chemistry, more tightly and squarely responsive to the immediate occasion, more purely the timbre and tremor of the electrocardiagraph made audible than can easily be found elsewhere. Even at the gravest moments the language never loses this extempore, unpredictable character of something being hurled together out of whatever verbal scrap happens to be lying around, everything within reach, snatched and grabbed out of the listener's ears, his shirt front, his top-pocket, in a crisis of effort to communicate not merely the full story but the human urgency of it and all its dramatic implications.

This sort of thing is part of the kit in all poetic medicine bags, but the Saturnalian disruptiveness and unorthodoxy of Shakespeare's procedure, as an accompaniment to his solemn themes, makes the eye and ear uniquely jumpy. One is aware of it as a signaling and hinting of verbal heads and tails both above and below precision, and by this weirdly expressive underswell of a musical near-gibberish, like a jostling of spirits, a bustling pressure of shapes inside every syllable. Shakespeare holds it all in dodgy focus by the auditory compass course that his aerobatic syntax plots through it. When Joyce takes this sonar amplification of the word's pun-possibilities to the limit in *Finnegans Wake,* the blazing crackle of radio interference and writhing wave bands somewhat smothers the instrument panel, for the reader and copilot, in a sort of whiteout. But by keeping all the voices aligned to the immediate challenge of one person speaking to another (and to that double audience) in the bracing crisis of action, Shakespeare turns those possibilities to his advantage. Without fogging the route, they amplify the consequences and significance of everything that happens. They evoke the heckling or sighing complicity of the background world, of the speaker's hidden being, teeming but obscure, and of other dimensions:

And when Love speaks the voice of all the gods
Makes Heaven drowsy with the harmony.

His language went through one more major change, as I mentioned before. In the last plays, which explore the salvation of the lost heroine and the redemption of the tragic hero, a new language appears. In this third language, the metaphorical density dissolves but the sense of complexity, and of packed, many-layered richness, remains. The complexity of knotted metaphor melts, that is, into a musical complexity, a sinuous, melodious orchestration of tones where words have resumed their simple directness without losing their amplitude. Again, this change corresponds to a major change in subject matter on the mythic level. The fatal collision of different worlds, dramatized in the tragedies proper, and in the compacted language of those plays, has been resolved in this new phase, where the hero, instead of causing the heroine's death and thereby bringing about his own, is reborn to her as she is to him. Their rebirth, wherever it occurs, is characterized by brimming passages of this new, simplified, yet enriched music, usually describing storm (the storm of death and rebirth) or flowers (the flowers of death and rebirth), or an ultimate transcendence. It first appears, briefly but unmistakably, in the scene that reunites Lear and Cordelia:

> No, no, no, no! Come, let's away to prison;
> We two alone will sing like birds i' the cage:
> When thou dost ask me blessing, I'll kneel down,
> And ask of thee forgiveness: so we'll live,
> And pray, and sing, and tell old tales, and laugh
> At gilded butterflies, and hear poor rogues
> Talk of court news; and we'll talk with them too,
> Who loses and who wins; who's in, who's out;
> And take upon's the mystery of things,
> As if we were God's spies: and we'll wear out,

> *In a wall'd prison, packs and sets of great ones*
> *That ebb and flow by the moon.*

And it suffuses the love scenes, particularly the love-death scenes, of *Antony and Cleopatra*. But it achieves its ultimate purity in the last four plays of the series. In *Pericles* the rebirth happens in a sea-storm. Pericles is casting his wife, who seems to have died in childbirth—but has not—into the sea in a sealed chest:

> *A terrible child-bed hast thou had, my dear;*
> *No light, no fire: the unfriendly elements*
> *Forgot thee utterly; nor have I time*
> *To give thee hallow'd to thy grave, but straight*
> *Must cast thee, scarcely coffin'd, in the ooze;*
> *Where, for a monument upon thy bones,*
> *And aye-remaining lamps, the belching whale*
> *And humming water must o'erwhelm thy corpse,*
> *Lying with simple shells!*

In *Cymbeline*, the rebirth happens in the funeral of Imogen (who is in a sleep like death), her brothers, who do not yet know they are her brothers, mourn her, supposing she is a boy, Fidele:

> *With fairest flowers*
> *While summer lasts and I live here, Fidele,*
> *I'll sweeten thy sad grave; thou shalt not lack*
> *The flower that's like thy face, pale primrose, nor*

The azur'd harebell, like thy veins, no, nor
The leaf of eglantine, whom not to slander,
Out-sweeten'd not thy breath: the ruddock would,
With charitable bill, — O bill! sore-shaming
Those rich-left heirs, that let their fathers lie
Without a monument, — bring thee all this;
Yea, and furr'd moss besides, when flowers are none,
To winter-ground thy corse.

In *The Winter's Tale,* the rebirth moment materializes with the first entry of Perdita, the shepherdess, as a flower queen, almost the Goddess Flora, in a prolonged flower ceremony:

I would I had some flowers o' the spring that might
Become your time of day; and yours, and yours,
That wear upon your virgin branches yet
Your maidenheads growing: O Proserpina!
For the flowers now that frighted thou let'st fall
From Dis's waggon! daffodils,
That come before the swallow dares, and take
The winds of March with beauty; violets dim,
But sweeter than the lids of Juno's eyes
Or Cytherea's breath; pale prime-roses,
That die unmarried, ere they can behold
Bright Phoebus in his strength, a malady
Most incident to maids.

while *The Tempest,* which can be called a drama of the ritual of this rebirth and the manageable (by magic) transcendence, is almost entirely composed in this new, lucent, aerial music.

These two principal changes in Shakespeare's poetic language, at *All's Well* and at the advent of transcendent rebirth, surmount and coexist with other, slighter—and in some cases not so slight—stylistic changes that seem to come with each new play. As he outgrows them (in other words, as he moves to the next play), these variations tend to remain as tones and textures in his repertoire, instruments in his orchestra, though wherever they recur they are always to some degree assimilated to the dominant poetry of that phase (just as in *The Tempest*, even the deliberately stilted, folk-play couplets of the masque are suffused with the mysterious, molten music of that final simplicity).

THE LANGUAGE of the Sonnets is different in kind from that of the plays. In the phantasmagoria of the plays, the language is egoless, provisional, a voice of many voices where each speech is made out of a sort of Protean ectoplasm that exudes from the peculiar living substance of each dramatis persona, an extension of the stuff of the world. It is also, as became clear in the king's speech from *All's Well*, a kind of algebra that explicates the physical and metaphysical universe of the particular play, and not only of that play but of Shakespeare's dramatic creation in general. (In this sense, the language of *The Tempest* is the algebraic language of the complete works, each statement loaded with referential meaning from all that has gone before, as if his whole oeuvre were a single work.) The consistency and integrity of this is Shakespeare's own, as if each play emerged, on a flow of large-minded inspiration, from Shakespeare's whole being. As the poet in *Timon of Athens* says in his poetic parable about the life and fall of a Timon: "A thing slipped idly from me." The controlling presence is not a discernible ego but an entire consciousness and life, a nation of selves.

In the Sonnets, in sharp contrast, the language is that of a very particular ego, the poet who wanted to make himself clear, man to man, in an especially urgent matter, as in a letter to a particular listener— Henry Wriothesley, his patron. Here Shakespeare speaks for himself, and is liable for what he says. If he is happy to lie, then he presumably accepts that his words will be meaningless. If he wants merely to amuse, then he must accept that he will be indulged only so far as he entertains, and that his credit will not go an inch further. These are modes to be avoided at all costs, though, if he has something to say that he wants his listener to believe. If he wants his listener to know that he loves him with real love, then he has to convince him. He has to prove it.

But Shakespeare knows, better than most, that mere words, outside any context of action, simply as statement, assertion, affirmation, or protestation, cannot prove anything. As Troilus says, tearing up the love letter from the unfaithful Cressida: "Words, words, mere words, no matter from the heart." Or as Timon says, dismissing Alcibiades's whores as incapable of anything but lying:

> *Although I know you'll swear, terribly swear,*
> *Into strong shudders and to heavenly agues*
> *The immortal gods that hear you.*

For most words, the problem never arises because they do not need to prove their truth. They know they cannot be expected to do more than suggest or assert. All true words labor under this patient shame — that the worst, most outrageous lies would make just as good a show, and could seize many immediate advantages. For their truth to become clear, true words have to wait for time, the world of action and trial, to supply a context and validate them, just as it will sweep away the lies. In the Sonnets, where the writer not only wants to make himself clear but also wants to prove, with words alone, like a man in the dock in court, immediately, his heart's truth, this is the central problem, and Shakespeare is aware of it as such — 300 years before the same problem brings philosophy to a halt.

In the plays, all the evidence is supplied, and the truth or falsehood of words can be assessed, if not immediately, at least by the end of the play, which completes an action that validates or fails to validate the words of all involved. But the Sonnets lack both the time, which could test them, and the immediate context of action, which could prove them. Therefore, the judge, Henry Wriothesley, as Shakespeare sees, can only suspend judgement. To lift his words beyond empty protestation, the best Shakespeare can do is to persuade his listener musically, by the tone of his voice. Poetry has a warrant for the office of truth-teller only insofar as its music becomes a form of action. And the music of a voice becomes action, and persuades us, only insofar as it persuades us on the level of intuitive empathy—the animal level. Obviously some ears are more intuitive than others, but it is common experience that in poetry (as in life), the tuning and cadence of the voice can persuade us to accept that the words are in some way true. Shakespeare, in his Sonnets, does this successfully, for very many readers. His music has this authority of the apparently authentic. It persuades us that his words are true. But we are sympathetic listeners perhaps. And he himself was suspicious of such music. He knew that the music of a voice is mainly a virtuosity of emphasis and mimicry.

Though he knew this, though he was, to a degree, obsessed with the knowledge that the heart's truth is inexpressible without some guarantee and down payment or indemnity on the physical plane, nevertheless, here in the courtroom dock of the Sonnets, his heart's truth was what he attempted to express. So he found himself, in a peculiar way, struck dumb.

A peculiar religious honesty locked up his words. This dumbness became a theme. In several sonnets, his ingenious eloquence plays around the insoluble, Wittgenstein-like dilemma. Other sonnets allude to it or assume it as a basic law. One can see him reaching for the other vocabulary of drama, a language made of objects simply as they are:

> *Who is it that says most? Which can say more*
> *Than this rich praise, that you alone are you?*

Or, half-joke, whole serious:

> *My mistress' eyes are nothing like the sun;*
> *Coral is far more red than her lips' red:*
> *If snow be white, why then her breasts are dun;*
> *If hairs be wires, black wires grow on her head.*

But his heart's truth, his "sacred love," the real god in his pantheon, remains, essentially, a "word within a word, unable to speak a word."

This circumstance helps to explain some things about the plays, and about their language, their verbal language, in particular. Not least, it illuminates the recurrent appearance of perfect simplicity, the simplicity which is closest to silence, as the highest ethical value—enshrined in his dramatic heroines, who bear and symbolize the ultimate suffering. So Cordelia is unable to find words for her heart's truth while, all around her, others are declaring what seems to be loyal, sincere love in haunting, musical cadences and lying words that will destroy them all.

This again, perhaps, helps to explain his penetration and clarity of mind. His "religious" honesty about the heart's truth can be seen as the obverse of his loathing of the lie. Maybe the one extreme is proportionate to the other. This loathing rises to a crescendo in *Timon of Athens,* where at the peak of Shakespeare's powers it shatters all dramatic constraints and pours out almost uncontrolled over Athens and audience alike. His near-pathological attitude toward falsity, and his corresponding truth to himself, have everything to do with the solidity of his words—the atoms from which he creates such a radiant and durable universe. His truth to his own nature is like a helplessness to be otherwise. In the Sonnets it sometimes appears as a kind of dismay, even as he accepts it:

> *Why is my verse so barren of new pride,*
> *So far from variation or quick change?*
> *Why, with the time, do I not glance aside*
> *To new-found methods and to compounds strange?*
> *Why write I still all one, ever the same,*
> *And keep invention in a noted weed,*
> *That every word doth almost tell my name,*
> *Showing their birth, and whence they did proceed?*
> *Oh know, sweet love, I always write of you,*
> *And you, and love, are still my argument;*

> *So all my best is dressing old words new,*
> *Spending again what is already spent:*
> > *For as the sun is daily new and old*
> > *So is my love still telling what is told.*

This plainness is not quite the plainness of Dryden
and the "middle style." It is something much more
subjectively aware: the psychological depth is in no
way sealed off. Not the plainness of a white marble
floor, but of bottomless, clear water, wide open and
immediate. As with a lens, the simple lucidity was
precisely what revealed the tremendous vision. That
same plainness, so alert internally, is the calm of
what—as he went on to prove—was both a perfect
fearlessness and an unflinching, total vulnerability.
The control and order of art are there, but none
of the defenses, none of the distancings and obliq-
uities. The nakedness of these poems embarrassed
W. H. Auden. The steadiness of the meter is like the
deliberation of a confrontation, a vigilance and a
focus. Confucius, presumably, would have admired
that clean, warm handclasp of word and fact. Help-
lessly honest, almost as a debility—but fearless to
face what that entails—and with a strength to fathom
and understand whatever consequences. Evidently
this is what enabled him to meet and come to grips
with such terrible internal events, bring them under
his control, and render such a full, humane, and im-
perishable account of them.

Like drama, these Sonnets, written as letters,

forced language back toward that norm, the language of the common bond, what Wordsworth called the language of "a man speaking to men." In Shakespeare's case, that language of the common bond was synthesized under a unique convergence of religious, political, and cultural extremes. It must be one of the most remarkable compound substances ever invented. One has to consider how far it enabled him to go, what he was able to construct with it, and, since then, what it has proved able to sustain. Maybe one can best examine its secrets and the temperament behind it, not in the later, composite structures of the great passages, but here in the "simple truth miscalled simplicity," the "true plain words by thy true-telling friend" of the Sonnets, which the sonneteer, dramatized in the figure of the deceived Troilus, regretted with:

> *Alas,*
> *I am as true as truth's simplicity*
> *And simpler than the infancy of truth.*

—*TED HUGHES*

SONNETS, SPEECHES, SONGS, AND POEMS

Music to hear, why hear'st thou music sadly?
Sweets with sweets war not, joy delights in joy:
Why lov'st thou that which thou receiv'st not gladly,
Or else receiv'st with pleasure thine annoy?
If the true concord of well-tuned sounds,
By unions married, do offend thine ear,
They do but sweetly chide thee, who confounds
In singleness the parts that thou shouldst bear.
Mark how one string, sweet husband to another,
Strikes each in each by mutual ordering;
Resembling sire and child and happy mother,
Who, all in one, one pleasing note do sing:
    Whose speechless song, being many, seeming one,
    Sings this to thee: "Thou single wilt prove none."

Now the hungry lion roars,
    And the wolf behowls the moon;

Whilst the heavy ploughman snores,
    All with weary task fordone,
Now the wasted brands do glow,
    Whilst the screech-owl, screeching loud,
Puts the wretch that lies in woe
    In remembrance of a shroud.
Now it is the time of night
    That the graves, all gaping wide,
Every one lets forth his sprite,
    In the church-way paths to glide:
And we fairies, that do run
    By the triple Hecate's team,
From the presence of the sun,
    Following darkness like a dream,
Now are frolic; not a mouse
Shall disturb this hallow'd house;
I am sent with broom before,
To sweep the dust behind the door.

Sin of self-love possesseth all mine eye
And all my soul and all my every part;
And for this sin there is no remedy,
It is so grounded inward in my heart.
Methinks no face so gracious is as mine,
No shape so true, no truth of such account;
And for myself mine own worth do define,
As I all other in all worths surmount.
But when my glass shows me myself indeed,

Beated and chopp'd with tann'd antiquity,
Mine own self-love quite contrary I read;
Self so self-loving were iniquity.
    'Tis thee, myself,— that for myself I praise,
    Painting my age with beauty of thy days.

Well, say there is no kingdom then for Richard;
What other pleasures can the world afford?
I'll make my heaven in a lady's lap,
And deck my body in gay ornaments,
And witch sweet ladies with my words and looks.
O miserable thought! and more unlikely
Than to accomplish twenty golden crowns.
Why, love forswore me in my mother's womb:
And, for I should not deal in her soft laws,
She did corrupt frail nature with some bribe,
To shrink mine arm up like a wither'd shrub;
To make an envious mountain on my back,
Where sits deformity to mock my body;
To shape my legs of an unequal size;
To disproportion me in every part,
Like to a chaos, or an unlick'd bear-whelp
That carries no impression like the dam.
And am I then a man to be belov'd?
O monstrous fault! to harbour such a thought.
Then, since this earth affords no joy to me
But to command, to check, to o'erbear such
As are of better person than myself,

I'll make my heaven to dream upon the crown;
And, whiles I live, to account this world but hell,
Until my mis-shap'd trunk that bears this head
Be round impaled with a glorious crown.
And yet I know not how to get the crown,
For many lives stand between me and home:
And I, like one lost in a thorny wood,
That rents the thorns and is rent with the thorns,
Seeking a way and straying from the way;
Not knowing how to find the open air,
But toiling desperately to find it out,
Torment myself to catch the English crown:
And from that torment I will free myself,
Or hew my way out with a bloody axe.
Why, I can smile, and murder while I smile,
And cry, "Content," to that which grieves my
    heart,
And wet my cheeks with artificial tears,
And frame my face to all occasions.
I'll drown more sailors than the mermaid shall;
I'll slay more gazers than the basilisk;
I'll play the orator as well as Nestor,
Deceive more slily than Ulysses could,
And, like a Sinon, take another Troy.
I can add colours to the chameleon,
Change shapes with Proteus for advantages,
And set the murd'rous Machiavel to school.
Can I do this, and cannot get a crown?
Tut! were it further off, I'll pluck it down.

Shall I compare thee to a summer's day?
Thou art more lovely and more temperate:
Rough winds do shake the darling buds of May,
And summer's lease hath all too short a date:
Sometime too hot the eye of heaven shines,
And often is his gold complexion dimm'd:
And every fair from fair sometime declines,
By chance, or nature's changing course untrimm'd;
But thy eternal summer shall not fade,
Nor lose possession of that fair thou ow'st,
Nor shall death brag thou wander'st in his shade,
When in eternal lines to time thou grow'st;
    So long as men can breathe, or eyes can see,
    So long lives this, and this gives life to thee.

But, soft! what light through yonder window breaks?
It is the east, and Juliet is the sun!
Arise, fair sun, and kill the envious moon,
Who is already sick and pale with grief,
That thou her maid art far more fair than she:
Be not her maid, since she is envious;
Her vestal livery is but sick and green,
And none but fools do wear it; cast it off.
It is my lady; O! it is my love:
O! that she knew she were.
She speaks, yet she says nothing: what of that?
Her eye discourses; I will answer it.

I am too bold, 'tis not to me she speaks:
Two of the fairest stars in all the heaven,
Having some business, do entreat her eyes
To twinkle in their spheres till they return.
What if her eyes were there, they in her head?
The brightness of her cheek would shame those
     stars
As daylight doth a lamp; her eyes in heaven
Would through the airy region stream so bright
That birds would sing and think it were not night.
See! how she leans her cheek upon her hand:
O! that I were a glove upon that hand,
That I might touch that cheek.

When I do count the clock that tells the time,
And see the brave day sunk in hideous night;
When I behold the violet past prime,
And sable curls, all silver'd o'er with white;
When lofty trees I see barren of leaves,
Which erst from heat did canopy the herd,
And summer's green all girded up in sheaves,
Borne on the bier with white and bristly beard,
Then of thy beauty do I question make,
That thou among the wastes of time must go,
Since sweets and beauties do themselves forsake
And die as fast as they see others grow;
     And nothing 'gainst Time's scythe can make
     defence

Save breed, to brave him when he takes thee hence.

I do affect the very ground, which is base, where her shoe, which is baser, guided by her foot, which is basest, doth tread. I shall be forsworn,—which is a great argument of falsehood,—if I love. And how can that be true love which is falsely attempted? Love is a familiar; Love is a devil: there is no evil angel but Love. Yet was Samson so tempted, and he had an excellent strength; yet was Solomon so seduced, and he had a very good wit. Cupid's butt-shaft is too hard for Hercules' club, and therefore too much odds for a Spaniard's rapier. The first and second clause will not serve my turn; the passado he respects not, the duello he regards not: his disgrace is to be called boy, but his glory is, to subdue men. Adieu, valour! rust, rapier! be still, drum! for your manager is in love; yea, he loveth. Assist me some extemporal god of rime, for I am sure I shall turn sonneter. Devise, wit; write, pen; for I am for whole volumes in folio.

But, lo! from forth a copse that neighbours by,
A breeding jennet, lusty, young, and proud,
Adonis' trampling courser doth espy,
And forth she rushes, snorts and neighs aloud:
    The strong-neck'd steed, being tied unto
    a tree,
    Breaketh his rein, and to her straight
    goes he.

Imperiously he leaps, he neighs, he bounds,
And now his woven girths he breaks asunder;
The bearing earth with his hard hoof he wounds,
Whose hollow womb resounds like heaven's
    thunder;
    The iron bit he crushes 'tween his teeth,
    Controlling what he was controlled with.

His ears up-prick'd; his braided hanging mane
Upon his compass'd crest now stand on end;
His nostrils drink the air, and forth again,
As from a furnace, vapours doth he send:
    His eye, which scornfully glisters like fire,
    Shows his hot courage and his high desire.

Sometime he trots, as if he told the steps,
With gentle majesty and modest pride;
Anon he rears upright, curvets and leaps,
As who should say, 'Lo! thus my strength is
    tried;
    And this I do to captivate the eye
    Of the fair breeder that is standing by.'

What recketh he his rider's angry stir,
His flattering 'Holla,' or his 'Stand, I say?'
What cares he now for curb or pricking spur?
For rich caparisons or trapping gay?
    He sees his love, and nothing else he sees,
    Nor nothing else with his proud sight
    agrees.

Look, when a painter would surpass the life,
In limning out a well-proportion'd steed,
His art with nature's workmanship at strife,
As if the dead the living should exceed;
    So did this horse excel a common one,
    In shape, in courage, colour, pace and bone.

Round-hoof'd, short-jointed, fetlocks shag and long,
Broad breast, full eye, small head, and nostril wide,
High crest, short ears, straight legs and passing
    strong,
Thin mane, thick tail, broad buttock, tender hide:
    Look, what a horse should have he did not lack,
    Save a proud rider on so proud a back.

Sometimes he scuds far off, and there he stares;
Anon he starts at stirring of a feather;
To bid the wind a race he now prepares,
And whe'r he run or fly they know not whether;
    For through his mane and tail the high wind
        sings,
    Fanning the hairs, who wave like feather'd
        wings.

He looks upon his love, and neighs unto her;
She answers him as if she knew his mind;
Being proud, as females are, to see him woo her,
She puts on outward strangeness, seems unkind,
    Spurns at his love and scorns the heat he feels,
    Beating his kind embracements with her heels.

Then, like a melancholy malcontent,
He vails his tail that, like a falling plume
Cool shadow to his melting buttock lent:
He stamps, and bites the poor flies in his fume.
    His love, perceiving how he is enrag'd,
    Grew kinder, and his fury was assuag'd.

His testy master goeth about to take him;
When lo! the unback'd breeder, full of fear,
Jealous of catching, swiftly doth forsake him,
With her the horse, and left Adonis there.
    As they were mad, unto the wood they hie
    them,
    Out-stripping crows that strive to over-fly them.

    I prophesy thy death, my living sorrow,
    If thou encounter with the boar to-morrow.

"But if thou needs wilt hunt, be rul'd by me;
Uncouple at the timorous flying hare,
Or at the fox which lives by subtilty,
Or at the roe which no encounter dare:
    Pursue these fearful creatures o'er the downs,
    And on thy well-breath'd horse keep with thy
    hounds.

"And when thou hast on foot the purblind hare,
Mark the poor wretch, to overshoot his troubles
How he outruns the winds, and with what care
He cranks and crosses with a thousand doubles:

The many musits through the which he goes
Are like a labyrinth to amaze his foes.

"Sometime he runs among a flock of sheep,
To make the cunning hounds mistake their smell,
And sometime where earth-delving conies keep,
To stop the loud pursuers in their yell,
   And sometime sorteth with a herd of deer;
   Danger deviseth shifts; wit waits on fear:

"For there his smell with others being mingled,
The hot scent-snuffing hounds are driven to doubt,
Ceasing their clamorous cry till they have singled
With much ado the cold fault cleanly out;
   Then do they spend their mouths: Echo replies,
   As if another chase were in the skies.

"By this, poor Wat, far off upon a hill,
Stands on his hinder legs with listening ear,
To hearken if his foes pursue him still:
Anon their loud alarums he doth hear;
   And now his grief may be compared well
   To one sore sick that hears the passing-bell.

"Then shalt thou see the dew-bedabbled wretch
Turn, and return, indenting with the way;
Each envious briar his weary legs doth scratch,
Each shadow makes him stop, each murmur stay:
   For misery is trodden on by many,
   And being low never reliev'd by any.

—Swearest thou, ungracious boy? henceforth ne'er look on me. Thou art violently carried away from grace: there is a devil haunts thee in the likeness of a fat old man; a tun of man is thy companion. Why dost thou converse with that trunk of humours, that bolting-hutch of beastliness, that swoln parcel of dropsies, that huge bombard of sack, that stuffed cloakbag of guts, that roasted Manningtree ox with the pudding in his belly, that reverend vice, that grey iniquity, that father ruffian, that vanity in years? Wherein is he good but to taste sack and drink it? wherein neat and cleanly but to carve a capon and eat it? wherein cunning but in craft? wherein crafty but in villany? wherein villainous but in all things? wherein worthy but in nothing?

—I would your Grace would take me with you: whom means your Grace?

—That villainous abominable misleader of youth, Falstaff, that old white-bearded Satan.

—My lord, the man I know.

—I know thou dost.

—But to say I know more harm in him than in myself were to say more than I know. That he is old, the more the pity, his white hairs do witness it; but that he is, saving your reverence, a whoremaster, that I utterly deny. If sack and sugar be a fault, God help the wicked! If to be old and merry be a sin, then many an old host that I know is damned: if to be fat be to be hated, then Pharaoh's lean kine are to be loved. No, my good lord; banish Peto, banish Bardolph, banish

Poins; but for sweet Jack Falstaff, kind Jack Falstaff, true Jack Falstaff, valiant Jack Falstaff, and therefore more valiant, being, as he is, old Jack Falstaff, banish not him thy Harry's company: banish not him thy Harry's company: banish plump Jack, and banish all the world.

—I do, I will.

Like as the waves make towards the pebbled shore,
So do our minutes hasten to their end;
Each changing place with that which goes before,
In sequent toil all forwards do contend.
Nativity, once in the main of light,
Crawls to maturity, wherewith being crown'd,
Crooked eclipses 'gainst his glory fight,
And Time that gave doth now his gift confound.
Time doth transfix the flourish set on youth
And delves the parallels in beauty's brow,
Feeds on the rarities of nature's truth,
And nothing stands but for his scythe to mow:
   And yet to times in hope my verse shall stand,
   Praising thy worth, despite his cruel hand.

I am amaz'd, methinks, and lose my way
Among the thorns and dangers of this world.
How easy dost thou take all England up!
From forth this morsel of dead royalty,
The life, the right and truth of all this realm

Is fled to heaven; and England now is left
To tug and scamble and to part by the teeth
The unow'd interest of proud swelling state.
Now for the bare-pick'd bone of majesty
Doth dogged war bristle his angry crest,
And snarleth in the gentle eyes of peace:
Now powers from home and discontents at home
Meet in one line; and vast confusion waits,—
As doth a raven on a sick-fallen beast,—
The imminent decay of wrested pomp.
Now happy he whose cloak and ceinture can
Hold out this tempest.

Not marble, nor the gilded monuments
Of princes, shall outlive this powerful rime;
But you shall shine more bright in these contents
Than unswept stone, besmear'd with sluttish time
When wasteful war shall statues overturn,
And broils root out of the work of masonry,
Nor Mars his sword nor war's quick fire shall burn
The living record of your memory.
'Gainst death and all-oblivious enmity
Shall you pace forth; your praise shall still find
    room
Even in the eyes of all posterity
That wear this world out to the ending doom.
    So, till the judgment that yourself arise,
    You live in this, and dwell in lovers' eyes.

But I remember, when the fight was done,
When I was dry with rage and extreme toil,
Breathless and faint, leaning upon my sword,
Came there a certain lord, neat, and trimly dress'd,
Fresh as a bridegroom; and his chin, new reap'd,
Show'd like a stubble-land at harvest-home:
He was perfumed like a milliner,
And 'twixt his finger and his thumb he held
A pouncet-box, which ever and anon
He gave his nose and took't away again;
Who therewith angry, when it next came there,
Took it in snuff: and still he smil'd and talk'd;
And as the soldiers bore dead bodies by,
He call'd them untaught knaves, unmannerly,
To bring a slovenly unhandsome corpse
Betwixt the wind and his nobility.
With many holiday and lady terms
He question'd me; among the rest, demanded
My prisoners in your majesty's behalf.
I then all smarting with my wounds being cold,
To be so pester'd with a popinjay,
Out of my grief and my impatience
Answer'd neglectingly, I know not what,
He should, or he should not; for he made me mad
To see him shine so brisk and smell so sweet
And talk so like a waiting-gentlewoman
Of guns, and drums, and wounds,—God save the
    mark!—
And telling me the sovereign'st thing on earth
Was parmaceti for an inward bruise;

And that it was great pity, so it was,
This villainous saltpetre should be digg'd
Out of the bowels of the harmless earth,
Which many a good tall fellow had destroy'd
So cowardly; and but for these vile guns,
He would himself have been a soldier.

Tir'd with all these, for restful death I cry
As to behold desert a beggar born,
And needy nothing trimm'd in jollity,
And purest faith unhappily forsworn,
And gilded honour shamefully misplac'd,
And maiden virtue rudely strumpeted,
And right perfection wrongfully disgraced,
And strength by limping sway disabled,
And art made tongue-tied by authority,
And folly—doctor-like—controlling skill,
And simple truth miscall'd simplicity,
And captive good attending captain ill:
    Tir'd with all these, from these would I be
    gone,
    Save that, to die, I leave my love alone.

Petruchio is coming, in a new hat and an old
jerkin; a pair of old breeches thrice turned; a pair
of boots that have been candle-cases, one buckled,
another laced; an old rusty sword ta'en out of the
town-armoury, with a broken hilt, and chapeless;

with two broken points: his horse hipped with an old
mothy saddle and stirrups of no kindred; besides,
possessed with the glanders and like to mose in the
chine; troubled with the lampass, infected with the
fashions, full of windgalls, sped with spavins, rayed
with the yellows, past cure of the fives, stark spoiled
with the staggers, begnawn with the bots, swayed
in the back, and shoulder-shotten; near-legged be-
fore, and with a half-checked bit, and a head-stall
of sheep's leather, which, being restrained to keep
him from stumbling, hath been often burst and now
repaired with knots; one girth six times pieced, and
a woman's crupper of velure, which hath two letters
for her name fairly set down in studs, and here and
there pieced with packthread.

Since brass, nor stone, nor earth, nor boundless sea,
But sad mortality o'ersways their power,
How with this rage shall beauty hold a plea,
Whose action is no stronger than a flower?
O! how shall summer's honey breath hold out
Against the wrackful siege of battering days,
When rocks impregnable are not so stout,
Nor gates of steel so strong, but Time decays?
O fearful meditation! where, alack,
Shall Time's best jewel from Time's chest lie hid?
Or what strong hand can hold his swift foot back?
Or who his spoil of beauty can forbid?
    O! none, unless this miracle have might,
    That in black ink my love may still shine bright.

Now hear our English king;
For thus his royalty doth speak in me.
He is prepar'd; and reason too he should:
This apish and unmannerly approach,
This harness'd masque and unadvised revel,
This unhair'd sauciness and boyish troops,
The king doth smile at; and is well prepar'd
To whip this dwarfish war, these pigmy arms,
From out the circle of his territories.
That hand which had the strength, even at your
    door,
To cudgel you and make you take the hatch;
To dive, like buckets, in concealed wells;
To crouch in litter of your stable planks;
To lie like pawns lock'd up in chests and trunks;
To hug with swine; to seek sweet safety out
In vaults and prisons; and to thrill and shake,
Even at the crying of your nation's crow,
Thinking this voice an armed Englishman:
Shall that victorious hand be feebled here
That in your chambers gave you chastisement?
No! Know, the gallant monarch is in arms,
And like an eagle o'er his aiery towers,
To souse annoyance that comes near his nest.
And you degenerate, you ingrate revolts,
You bloody Neroes, ripping up the womb
Of your dear mother England, blush for shame:
    For your own ladies and pale-visag'd maids
    Like Amazons come tripping after drums,
    Their thimbles into armed gauntlets change,

Their needl's to lances, and their gentle hearts
To fierce and bloody inclination.

No more be griev'd at that which thou hast done:
Roses have thorns, and silver fountains mud;
Clouds and eclipses stain both moon and sun,
And loathsome canker lives in sweetest bud.
All men make faults, and even I in this,
Authorising thy trespass with compare,
Myself corrupting, salving thy amiss,
Excusing thy sins more than thy sins are;
For to thy sensual fault I bring in sense,—
Thy adverse party is thy advocate,—
And 'gainst myself a lawful plea commence:
Such civil war is in my love and hate,
    That I an accessary needs must be
    To that sweet thief which sourly robs from me.

That very time I saw, but thou couldst not,
Flying between the cold moon and the earth,
Cupid all arm'd: a certain aim he took
At a fair vestal throned by the west,
And loos'd his love-shaft smartly from his bow,
As it should pierce a hundred thousand hearts;
But I might see young Cupid's fiery shaft
Quench'd in the chaste beams of the wat'ry moon,

And the imperial votaress passed on,
In maiden meditation, fancy-free.
Yet mark'd I where the bolt of Cupid fell:
It fell upon a little western flower,
Before milk-white, now purple with love's wound,
And maidens call it, Love-in-idleness.
Fetch me that flower; the herb I show'd thee once:
The juice of it on sleeping eyelids laid
Will make or man or woman madly dote
Upon the next live creature that it sees.
Fetch me this herb.

—Bless our poor virginity from underminers and blowers up! Is there no military policy, how virgins might blow up men?

—Virginity being blown down, man will quicklier be blown up: marry in blowing him down again, with the breach yourselves made, you lose your city. It is not politic in the commonwealth of nature to preserve virginity. Loss of virginity is rational increase, and there was never virgin got till virginity was first lost. That you were made of is metal to make virgins. Virginity, by being once lost, may be ten times found: by being ever kept, it is ever lost. 'Tis too cold a companion: away with't!

—I will stand for't a little, though therefore I die a virgin.

—There's little can be said in't; 'tis against the rule of nature. To speak on the part of virginity is to accuse your mothers, which is most infallible disobedience.

He that hangs himself is a virgin: virginity murders itself, and should be buried in highways, out of all sanctified limit, as a desperate offendress against nature. Virginity breeds mites, much like a cheese, consumes itself to the very paring, and so dies with feeding his own stomach. Besides, virginity is peevish, proud, idle, made of self-love, which is the most inhibited sin in the canon. Keep it not; you cannot choose but lose by't! Out with't! within the year it will make itself two, which is a goodly increase, and the principal itself not much the worse. Away with't!

—How might one do, sir, to lose it to her own liking?

—Let me see: marry, ill, to like him that ne'er it likes. 'Tis a commodity that will lose the gloss with lying; the longer kept, the less worth: off with't, while 'tis vendible; answer the time of request. Virginity, like an old courtier, wears her cap out of fashion; richly suited, but unsuitable: just like the brooch and the toothpick, which wear not now. Your date is better in your pie and your porridge than in your cheek; and your virginity, your old virginity, is like one of our French withered pears; it looks ill, it eats drily; marry, 'tis a withered pear; it was formerly better; marry, yet 'tis a withered pear. Will you anything with it?

Let those who are in favour with their stars
Of public honour and proud titles boast,
Whilst I, whom fortune of such triumph bars,
Unlook'd for joy in that I honour most.

Great princes' favourites their fair leaves spread
But as the marigold at the sun's eye,
And in themselves their pride lies buried,
For at a frown they in their glory die.
The painful warrior famoused for fight,
After a thousand victories once foil'd,
Is from the book of honour razed quite,
And all the rest forgot for which he toil'd:
    Then happy I, that love and am belov'd,
    Where I may not remove nor be remov'd.

I cannot tell what you and other men
Think of this life; but, for my single self,
I had as lief not be as live to be
In awe of such a thing as I myself.
I was born free as Cæsar; so were you:
We both have fed as well, and we can both
Endure the winter's cold as well as he:
For once, upon a raw and gusty day,
The troubled Tiber chafing with her shores,
Cæsar said to me, "Dar'st thou, Cassius, now
Leap in with me into this angry flood,
And swim to yonder point?" Upon the word,
Accoutred as I was, I plunged in
And bade him follow; so, indeed he did.
The torrent roar'd, and we did buffet it
With lusty sinews, throwing it aside
And stemming it with hearts of controversy;

But ere we could arrive the point propos'd,
Cæsar cried, "Help me, Cassius, or I sink!"
I, as Æneas, our great ancestor,
Did from the flames of Troy upon his shoulder
The old Anchises bear, so from the waves of Tiber
Did I the tired Cæsar. And this man
Is now become a god, and Cassius is
A wretched creature and must bend his body
If Cæsar carelessly but nod on him.
He had a fever when he was in Spain,
And when the fit was on him, I did mark
How he did shake; 'tis true, this god did shake
His coward lips did from their colour fly,
And that same eye whose bend doth awe the world
Did lose his lustre; I did hear him groan;
Ay, and that tongue of his that bade the Romans
Mark him and write his speeches in their books,
Alas! it cried, "Give me some drink, Titinius,"
As a sick girl. Ye gods, it doth amaze me,
A man of such a feeble temper should
So get the start of the majestic world,
And bear the palm alone.

Devouring Time, blunt thou the lion's paws,
And make the earth devour her own sweet brood;
Pluck the keen teeth from the fierce tiger's jaws,
And burn the long-liv'd phoenix in her blood;
Make glad and sorry seasons as thou fleet'st,

And do whate'er thou wilt, swift-footed Time,
To the wide world and all her fading sweets;
But I forbid thee one most heinous crime:
O! carve not with thy hours my love's fair brow,
Nor draw no lines there with thine antique pen;
Him in thy course untainted do allow
For beauty's pattern to succeeding men.
    Yet, do thy worst, old Time: despite thy wrong,
    My love shall in my verse ever live young.

A fool, a fool! I met a fool i' the forest,
A motley fool; a miserable world!
As I do live by food, I met a fool;
Who laid him down and bask'd him in the sun,
And rail'd on Lady Fortune in good terms,
In good set terms, and yet a motley fool.
"Good morrow, fool," quoth I. "No, sir," quoth he,
"Call me not fool till heaven hath sent me fortune."
And then he drew a dial from his poke,
And, looking on it with lack-lustre eye,
Says very wisely, "It is ten o'clock;
Thus may we see," quoth he, "how the world wags:
'Tis but an hour ago since it was nine,
And after one hour more 'twill be eleven;
And so from hour to hour we ripe and ripe,
And then from hour to hour we rot and rot,
And thereby hangs a tale." When I did hear
The motley fool thus moral on the time,

My lungs began to crow like chanticleer,
That fools should be so deep-contemplative,
And I did laugh sans intermission
An hour by his dial. O noble fool!
A worthy fool! Motley's the only wear.

That time of year thou mayst in me behold
When yellow leaves, or none, or few, do hang
Upon those boughs which shake against the cold,
Bare ruin'd choirs, where late the sweet birds sang.
In me thou see'st the twilight of such day
As after sunset fadeth in the west;
Which by and by black night doth take away,
Death's second self, that seals up all in rest.
In me thou see'st the glowing of such fire,
That on the ashes of his youth doth lie,
As the death-bed whereon it must expire
Consum'd with that which it was nourish'd by.
   This thou perceiv'st, which makes thy love more
   strong,
   To love that well which thou must leave ere
   long.

I have been studying how I may compare
This prison where I live unto the world:
And for because the world is populous,

And here is not a creature but myself,
I cannot do it; yet I'll hammer it out.
My brain I'll prove the female to my soul;
My soul the father: and these two beget
A generation of still-breeding thoughts,
And these same thoughts people this little world
In humours like the people of this world.
For no thought is contented. The better sort,
As thoughts of things divine, are intermix'd
With scruples, and do set the word itself
Against the word:
As thus, "Come, little ones;" and then again,
"It is as hard to come as for a camel
To thread the postern of a needle's eye."
Thoughts tending to ambition, they do plot
Unlikely wonders; how these vain weak nails
May tear a passage through the flinty ribs
Of this hard world, my ragged prison walls;
And, for they cannot, die in their own pride.
Thoughts tending to content flatter themselves
That they are not the first of fortune's slaves,
Nor shall not be the last; like silly beggars
Who sitting in the stocks refuge their shame,
That many have and others must sit there:
And in this thought they find a kind of ease,
Bearing their own misfortune on the back
Of such as have before endur'd the like.
Thus play I in one person many people,
And none contented: sometimes am I king;
Then treason makes me wish myself a beggar,

And so I am: then crushing penury
Persuades me I was better when a king;
Then am I king'd again; and by and by
Think that I am unking'd by Bolingbroke,
And straight am nothing: but whate'er I be,
Nor I nor any man that but man is
With nothing shall be pleas'd, till he be eas'd
With being nothing.

They that have power to hurt and will do none,
That do not do the thing they most do show,
Who, moving others, are themselves as stone,
Unmoved, cold, and to temptation slow;
They rightly do inherit heaven's graces,
And husband nature's riches from expense;
They are the lords and owners of their faces,
Others but stewards of their excellence.
The summer's flower is to the summer sweet,
Though to itself it only live and die,
But if that flower with base infection meet,
The basest weed outbraves his dignity:
    For sweetest things turn sourest by their deeds;
    Lilies that fester smell far worse than weeds.

Good faith, this same young sober-blooded boy
doth not love me; nor a man cannot make him laugh;
but that's no marvel, he drinks no wine. There's
never none of these demure boys come to any proof;

for thin drink doth so over-cool their blood, and making many fish-meals, that they fall into a kind of male green-sickness; and then, when they marry, they get wenches. They are generally fools and cowards, which some of us should be too but for inflammation. A good sherris-sack hath a two-fold operation in it. It ascends me into the brain; dries me there all the foolish and dull and crudy vapours which environ it; makes it apprehensive, quick, forgetive, full of nimble, fiery, and delectable shapes; which, deliver'd o'er to the voice, the tongue, which is the birth, becomes excellent wit. The second property of your excellent sherris is, the warming of the blood; which, before cold and settled, left the liver white and pale, which is the badge of pusillanimity and cowardice: but the sherris warms it and makes it course from the inwards to the parts extreme. It illumineth the face, which, as a beacon, gives warning to all the rest of this little kingdom, man, to arm; and then the vital commoners and inland petty spirits muster me all to their captain, the heart, who, great and puffed up with this retinue, doth any deed of courage; and this valour comes of sherris. So that skill in the weapon is nothing without sack, for that sets it a-work; and learning, a mere hoard of gold kept by a devil till sack commences it and sets it in act and use. Hereof comes it that Prince Harry is valiant; for the cold blood he did naturally inherit of his father, he hath, like lean, sterile, and bare land, manured, husbanded, and tilled, with excellent endeavour of drinking good and good store of fertile sherris, that he is become very hot and valiant. If I had a thousand sons, the first human principle I would teach them should be, to forswear thin potations and to addict themselves to sack.

If music be the food of love, play on;
Give me excess of it, that, surfeiting,
The appetite may sicken, and so die.
That strain again! it had a dying fall:
O! it came o'er my ear like the sweet sound
That breathes upon a bank of violets,
Stealing and giving odour. Enough! no more:
'Tis not so sweet now as it was before.
O spirit of love! how quick and fresh art thou,
That, notwithstanding thy capacity
Receiveth as the sea, nought enters there,
Of what validity and pitch soe'er,
But falls into abatement and low price,
Even in a minute: so full of shapes is fancy,
That it alone is high fantastical.

My tongue-tied Muse in manners holds her still,
Whilst comments of your praise, richly compil'd,
Reserve their character with golden quill,
And precious phrase by all the Muses fil'd.
I think good thoughts, while others write good
    words,

And, like unletter'd clerk, still cry "Amen"
To every hymn that able spirit affords,
In polish'd form of well-refined pen.
Hearing you prais'd, I say, " 'Tis so, 'tis true,"
And to the most of praise add something more;
But that is in my thought, whose love to you,
Though words come hindmost, holds his rank
　　before.
　　Then others for the breath of words respect,
　　Me for my dumb thoughts, speaking in effect.

　　Come away, come away, death,
　　　　And in sad cypress let me be laid;
Fly away, fly away, breath;
　　　　I am slain by a fair cruel maid.
My shroud of white, stuck all with yew,
　　　　　　O! prepare it.
My part of death, no one so true
　　　　　　Did share it.

Not a flower, not a flower sweet,
　　　　On my black coffin let there be strown;
Not a friend, not a friend greet
　　　　My poor corse, where my bones shall be thrown.
A thousand thousand sighs to save,
　　　　　　Lay me, O! where
Sad true lover never find my grave,
　　　　　　To weep there.

But be contented: when that fell arrest
Without all bail shall carry me away,
My life hath in this line some interest,
Which for memorial still with thee shall stay.
When thou reviewest this, thou dost review
The very part was consecrate to thee:
The earth can have but earth, which is his due;
My spirit is thine, the better part of me:
So then thou hast but lost the dregs of life,
The prey of worms, my body being dead;
The coward conquest of a wretch's knife,
Too base of thee to be remembered.
    The worth of that is that which it contains,
    And that is this, and this with thee remains.

For do but note a wild and wanton herd,
Or race of youthful and unhandled colts,
Fetching mad bounds, bellowing and neighing
    loud,
Which is the hot condition of their blood;
If they but hear perchance a trumpet sound,
Or any air of music touch their ears,
You shall perceive them make a mutual stand,
Their savage eyes turn'd to a modest gaze
By the sweet power of music: therefore the poet
Did feign that Orpheus drew trees, stones, and
    floods;
Since nought so stockish, hard, and full of rage,

But music for the time doth change his nature.
The man that hath no music in himself,
Nor is not mov'd with concord of sweet sounds,
Is fit for treasons, stratagems, and spoils;
The motions of his spirit are dull as night,
And his affections dark as Erebus:
Let no such man be trusted. Mark the music.

Farewell! thou art too dear for my possessing,
And like enough thou know'st thy estimate:
The charter of thy worth gives thee releasing;
My bonds in thee are all determinate.
For how do I hold thee but by thy granting?
And for that riches where is my deserving?
The cause of this fair gift in me is wanting,
And so my patent back again is swerving.
Thyself thou gav'st, thy own worth then not
    knowing,
Or me, to whom thou gav'st it, else mistaking;
So thy great gift, upon misprision growing,
Comes home again, on better judgment making.
    Thus have I had thee, as a dream doth flatter,
    In sleep a king, but, waking, no such matter.

Are not these woods
More free from peril than the envious court?

Here feel we but the penalty of Adam,
The seasons' difference; as, the icy fang
And churlish chiding of the winter's wind,
Which, when it bites and blows upon my body,
Even till I shrink with cold, I smile and say
"This is no flattery: these are counsellors
That feelingly persuade me what I am."
Sweet are the uses of adversity,
Which like the toad, ugly and venomous,
Wears yet a precious jewel in his head;
And this our life exempt from public haunt,
Finds tongues in trees, books in the running brooks,
Sermons in stones, and good in every thing.

Was it the proud full sail of his great verse,
Bound for the prize of all too precious you,
That did my ripe thoughts in my brain inhearse,
Making their tomb the womb wherein they grew?
Was it his spirit, by spirits taught to write
Above a mortal pitch, that struck me dead?
No, neither he, nor his compeers by night
Giving him aid, my verse astonished.
He, nor that affable familiar ghost
Which nightly gulls him with intelligence,
As victors of my silence cannot boast;
I was not sick of any fear from thence:
    But when your countenance fill'd up his line,
    Then lack'd I matter; that enfeebled mine.

Now is the winter of our discontent
Made glorious summer by this sun of York;
And all the clouds that lour'd upon our house
In the deep bosom of the ocean buried.
Now are our brows bound with victorious wreaths;
Our bruised arms hung up for monuments;
Our stern alarums changed to merry meetings;
Our dreadful marches to delightful measures.
Grim-visag'd war hath smooth'd his wrinkled
    front;
And now,—instead of mounting barbed steeds,
To fright the souls of fearful adversaries,—
He capers nimbly in a lady's chamber
To the lascivious pleasing of a lute.
But I, that am not shap'd for sportive tricks,
Nor made to court an amorous looking-glass;
I, that am rudely stamp'd, and want love's majesty
To strut before a wanton ambling nymph;
I, that am curtail'd of this fair proportion,
Cheated of feature by dissembling nature,
Deform'd, unfinish'd, sent before my time
Into this breathing world, scarce half made up,
And that so lamely and unfashionable
That dogs bark at me, as I halt by them;
Why, I, in this weak piping time of peace,
Have no delight to pass away the time,
Unless to see my shadow in the sun
And descant on mine own deformity:
And therefore, since I cannot prove a lover,

To entertain these fair well-spoken days,
I am determined to prove a villain,
And hate the idle pleasures of these days.

Then hate me when thou wilt; if ever, now;
Now, while the world is bent my deeds to cross,
Join with the spite of fortune, make me bow,
And do not drop in for an after-loss:
Ah! do not, when my heart hath 'scap'd this
    sorrow,
Come in the rearward of a conquer'd woe;
Give not a windy night a rainy morrow,
To linger out a purpos'd overthrow.
If thou wilt leave me, do not leave me last,
When other petty griefs have done their spite,
But in the onset come: so shall I taste
At first the very worst of fortune's might;
    And other strains of woe, which now seem woe,
    Compar'd with loss of thee will not seem so.

When a man's servant shall play the cur with him,
look you, it goes hard; one that I brought up of a
puppy; one that I saved from drowning, when three
or four of his blind brothers and sisters went to it.
I have taught him, even as one would say precisely,
"Thus would I teach a dog." I was sent to deliver him
as a present to Mistress Silvia from my master, and I

came no sooner into the dining-chamber but he steps me to her trencher and steals her capon's leg. O! 'tis a foul thing when a cur cannot keep himself in all companies. I would have, as one should say, one that takes upon him to be a dog indeed, to be, as it were, a dog at all things. If I had not had more wit than he, to take a fault upon me that he did, I think verily he had been hanged for't: sure as I live, he had suffered for't: you shall judge. He thrusts me himself into the company of three or four gentleman-like dogs under the duke's table: he had not been there—bless the mark—a pissing-while, but all the chamber smelt him. "Out with the dog!" says one; "What cur is that?" says another; "Whip him out," says the third; "Hang him up," says the duke. I, having been acquainted with the smell before, knew it was Crab, and goes me to the fellow that whips the dogs: "Friend," quoth I, "you mean to whip the dog?" "Ay, marry, do I," quoth he. "You do him the more wrong," quoth I; " 'twas I did the thing you wot of." He makes me no more ado, but whips me out of the chamber. How many masters would do this for his servant? Nay, I'll be sworn, I have sat in the stocks for puddings he hath stolen, otherwise he had been executed; I have stood on the pillory for geese he hath killed, otherwise he had suffered for't; thou thinkest not of this now. Nay, I remember the trick you served me when I took my leave of Madam Silvia: did not I bid thee still mark me and do as I do? When didst thou see me heave up my leg and make water against a

gentlewoman's farthingale? Didst thou ever see me
do such a trick?

Say that thou didst forsake me for some fault,
And I will comment upon that offence:
Speak of my lameness, and I straight will halt,
Against thy reasons making no defence.
Thou canst not, love, disgrace me half so ill,
To set a form upon desired change,
As I'll myself disgrace; knowing thy will,
I will acquaintance strangle, and look strange;
Be absent from thy walks; and in my tongue
Thy sweet beloved name no more shall dwell,
Lest I, too much profane, should do it wrong,
And haply of our old acquaintance tell.
    For thee, against myself I'll vow debate,
    For I must ne'er love him whom thou dost hate.

Blow, blow, thou winter wind,
Thou art not so unkind
    As man's ingratitude;
Thy tooth is not so keen,
Because thou art not seen,
    Although thy breath be rude.
Heigh-ho! sing, heigh-ho! unto the green holly:
Most friendship is feigning, most loving mere folly.
    Then heigh-ho! the holly!
      This life is most jolly.

Freeze, freeze, thou bitter sky,
That dost not bite so nigh
  As benefits forgot:
Though thou the waters warp,
Thy sting is not so sharp
  As friend remember'd not.
Heigh-ho! sing, heigh-ho! unto the green holly:
Most friendship is feigning, most loving mere
 folly.
  Then heigh-ho! the holly!
   This life is most jolly.

When to the sessions of sweet silent thought
I summon up remembrance of things past,
I sigh the lack of many a thing I sought,
And with old woes new wail my dear times'
 waste:
Then can I drown an eye, unus'd to flow,
For precious friends hid in death's dateless
 night,
And weep afresh love's long since cancell'd woe,
And moan the expense of many a vanish'd sight:
Then can I grieve at grievances foregone,
And heavily from woe to woe tell o'er
The sad account of fore-bemoaned moan,
Which I new pay as if not paid before.
  But if the while I think on thee, dear friend,
  All losses are restor'd and sorrows end.

Lovers and madmen have such seething brains,
Such shaping fantasies, that apprehend
More than cool reason ever comprehends.
The lunatic, the lover, and the poet,
Are of imagination all compact:
One sees more devils than vast hell can hold,
That is, the madman; the lover, all as frantic,
Sees Helen's beauty in a brow of Egypt:
The poet's eye, in a fine frenzy rolling,
Doth glance from heaven to earth, from earth to
    heaven;
And, as imagination bodies forth
The forms of things unknown, the poet's pen
Turns them to shapes, and gives to airy nothing
A local habitation and a name.
Such tricks hath strong imagination,
That, if it would but apprehend some joy,
It comprehends some bringer of that joy;
Or in the night, imagining some fear,
How easy is a bush suppos'd a bear!

My love is strengthen'd, though more weak in
    seeming;
I love not less, though less the show appear:
That love is merchandiz'd whose rich esteeming
The owner's tongue doth publish everywhere.
Our love was new, and then but in the spring,
When I was wont to greet it with my lays;

Have you not heard it said full oft,
A woman's nay doth stand for nought?

Think, women love to match with men
And not to live so like a saint:
Here is no heaven; they holy then
Begin when age doth them attaint.
    Were kisses all the joys in bed,
    One woman would another wed.

But, soft! enough! too much, I fear;
For if my mistress hear my song,
She will not stick to ring my ear,
To teach my tongue to be so long:
    Yet will she blush, here be it said,
    To hear her secrets so bewray'd.

Love is too young to know what conscience is;
Yet who knows not conscience is born of love?
Then, gentle cheater, urge not my amiss,
Lest guilty of my faults thy sweet self prove:
For, thou betraying me, I do betray
My nobler part to my gross body's treason;
My soul doth tell my body that he may
Triumph in love; flesh stays no further
    reason,
But rising at thy name doth point out thee

As his triumphant prize. Proud of this pride,
He is contented thy poor drudge to be,
To stand in thy affairs, fall by thy side.
     No want of conscience hold it that I call
     Her "love" for whose dear love I rise and fall.

It was a lover and his lass,
     With a hey, and a ho, and a hey nonino,
That o'er the green corn-field did pass,
     In the spring time, the only pretty ring time,
When birds do sing, hey ding a ding, ding;
Sweet lovers love the spring.

Between the acres of the rye,
     With a hey, and a ho, and a hey nonino,
These pretty country folks would lie,
     In the spring time, &c.

This carol they began that hour,
     With a hey, and a ho, and a hey nonino,
How that a life was but a flower
     In the spring time, &c.

And therefore take the present time,
     With a hey, and a ho, and a hey nonino;
For love is crowned with the prime
     In the spring time, &c.

The forward violet thus did I chide:
Sweet thief, whence didst thou steal thy sweet that
    smells,
If not from my love's breath? The purple pride
Which on thy soft cheek for complexion dwells
In my love's veins thou hast too grossly dy'd.
The lily I condemned for thy hand,
And buds of marjoram had stol'n thy hair;
The roses fearfully on thorns did stand,
One blushing shame, another white despair;
A third, nor red nor white, had stol'n of both,
And to his robbery had annex'd thy breath;
But, for his theft, in pride of all his growth
A vengeful canker eat him up to death.
    More flowers I noted, yet I none could see
    But sweet or colour it had stol'n from thee.

Forsooth, in love! I, that have been love's whip;
A very beadle to a humorous sigh;
A critic, nay, a night-watch constable,
A domineering pedant o'er the boy,
Than whom no mortal so magnificent!
This wimpled, whining, purblind, wayward boy,
This senior-junior, giant-dwarf, Dan Cupid;
Regent of love-rimes, lord of folded arms,
The anointed sovereign of sighs and groans,
Liege of all loiterers and malecontents,
Dread prince of plackets, king of codpieces,

Sole imperator and great general
Of trotting 'paritors: O my little heart!
And I to be a corporal of his field,
And wear his colours like a tumbler's hoop!
What I! I love! I sue! I seek a wife!
A woman that is like a German clock,
Still a-repairing, ever out of frame,
And never going aright, being a watch,
But being watch'd that it may still go right!
Nay, to be perjur'd, which is worst of all;
And, among three, to love the worst of all;
A wightly wanton with a velvet brow,
With two pitch balls stuck in her face for eyes;
Ay, and, by heaven, one that will do the deed
Though Argus were her eunuch and her guard:
And I to sigh for her! to watch for her!
To pray for her! Go to; it is a plague
That Cupid will impose for my neglect
Of his almighty dreadful little might.
Well I will love, write, sigh, pray, sue, and groan:
Some men must love my lady, and some Joan.

What's in the brain, that ink may character,
Which hath not figur'd to thee my true spirit?
What's new to speak, what new to register,
That may express my love, or thy dear merit?
Nothing, sweet boy; but yet, like prayers divine,
I must each day say o'er the very same;

Counting no old thing old, thou mine, I thine,
Even as when first I hallow'd thy fair name.
So that eternal love in love's fresh case
Weighs not the dust and injury of age,
Nor gives to necessary wrinkles place,
But makes antiquity for aye his page;
    Finding the first conceit of love there bred,
    Where time and outward form would show it
    dead.

O mistress mine! where are you roaming?
O! stay and hear; your true love's coming,
    That can sing both high and low.
Trip no further, pretty sweeting;
Journeys end in lovers meeting,
    Every wise man's son doth know.

What is love? 'tis not hereafter;
Present mirth hath present laughter;
    What's to come is still unsure:
In delay there lies no plenty;
Then come kiss me, sweet and twenty,
    Youth's a stuff will not endure.

Let not my love be call'd idolatry,
Nor my beloved as an idol show,

Since all alike my songs and praises be
To one, of one, still such, and ever so.
Kind is my love to-day, to-morrow kind,
Still constant in a wondrous excellence;
Therefore my verse, to constancy confin'd,
One thing expressing, leaves out difference.
"Fair, kind, and true," is all my argument,
"Fair, kind, and true," varying to other words;
And in this change is my invention spent,
Three themes in one, which wondrous scope
    affords.
    "Fair, kind, and true," have often liv'd alone,
    Which three till now never kept seat in one.

—Methought that I had broken from the Tower,
And was embark'd to cross to Burgundy;
And in my company my brother Gloucester,
Who from my cabin tempted me to walk
Upon the hatches: hence we look'd toward
    England,
And cited up a thousand heavy times,
During the wars of York and Lancaster,
That had befall'n us. As we pac'd along
Upon the giddy footing of the hatches,
Methought that Gloucester stumbled; and, in
    falling,
Struck me, that thought to stay him, overboard,
Into the tumbling billows of the main.

Lord, Lord! methought what pain it was to drown:
What dreadful noise of water in mine ears!
What sights of ugly death within mine eyes!
Methought I saw a thousand fearful wracks;
A thousand men that fishes gnaw'd upon;
Wedges of gold, great anchors, heaps of pearl,
Inestimable stones, unvalu'd jewels,
All scatter'd in the bottom of the sea.
Some lay in dead men's skulls; and in those holes
Where eyes did once inhabit, there were crept,
As 'twere in scorn of eyes, reflecting gems,
That woo'd the slimy bottom of the deep,
And mock'd the dead bones that lay scatter'd by.
  —Had you such leisure in the time of death.
To gaze upon those secrets of the deep?
  —Methought I had; and often did I strive
To yield the ghost; but still the envious flood
Stopt in my soul, and would not let it forth
To find the empty, vast, and wandering air;
But smother'd it within my panting bulk,
Which almost burst to belch it in the sea.
  —Awak'd you not with this sore agony?
  —No, no, my dream was lengthen'd after life;
O! then began the tempest to my soul.
I pass'd, methought, the melancholy flood,
With that grim ferryman which poets write of,
Unto the kingdom of perpetual night.
The first that there did greet my stranger soul,
Was my great father-in-law, renowned Warwick;
Who cried aloud, "What scourge for perjury

Can this dark monarchy afford false Clarence?"
And so he vanish'd: then came wandering by
A shadow like an angel, with bright hair
Dabbled in blood; and he shriek'd out aloud,
"Clarence is come,—false, fleeting, perjur'd
　　Clarence,
That stabb'd me in the field by Tewksbury;—
Seize on him! Furies, take him unto torment."
With that, methought, a legion of foul fiends
Environ'd me, and howled in mine ears
Such hideous cries, that, with the very noise
I trembling wak'd, and, for a season after
Could not believe but that I was in hell,
Such terrible impression made my dream.

　　Nay, sure, he's not in hell: he's in Arthur's bosom,
if ever man went to Arthur's bosom. A' made a finer
end and went away an it had been any christom child;
a' parted even just between twelve and one, even at
the turning o' the tide: for after I saw him fumble
with the sheets and play with flowers and smile upon
his fingers' ends, I knew there was but one way; for his
nose was as sharp as a pen, and a' babbled of green
fields. "How now, Sir John!" quoth I: "what man! be
of good cheer." So a' cried out "God, God, God!"
three or four times: now I, to comfort him, bid him a'
should not think of God, I hoped there was no need
to trouble himself with any such thoughts yet. So a'
bade me lay more clothes on his feet: I put my hand
into the bed and felt them, and they were as cold as

any stone; then I felt to his knees, and so upward, and upward, and all was as cold as any stone.

Some glory in their birth, some in their skill,
Some in their wealth, some in their body's force;
Some in their garments, though new-fangled ill;
Some in their hawks and hounds, some in their
    horse;
And every humour hath his adjunct pleasure,
Wherein it finds a joy above the rest:
But these particulars are not my measure;
All these I better in one general best.
Thy love is better than high birth to me,
Richer than wealth, prouder than garments'
    cost,
Of more delight than hawks or horses be;
And having thee, of all men's pride I boast:
    Wretched in this alone, that thou mayst take
    All this away, and me most wretched make.

Spring

I

When daisies pied and violets blue
    And lady-smocks all silver-white
And cuckoo-buds of yellow hue
    Do paint the meadows with delight,
The cuckoo then, on every tree,

Mocks married men; for thus sings he,
                              Cuckoo;
Cuckoo, cuckoo: O, word of fear,
Unpleasing to a married ear!

II

When shepherds pipe on oaten straws,
    And merry larks are ploughmen's clocks,
When turtles tread, and rooks, and daws,
    And maidens bleach their summer smocks,
The cuckoo then, on every tree,
Mocks married men; for thus sings he,
                              Cuckoo;
Cuckoo, cuckoo: O, word of fear,
Unpleasing to a married ear!

Winter

III

When icicles hang by the wall,
    And Dick the shepherd blows his nail,
And Tom bears logs into the hall,
    And milk comes frozen home in pail,
When blood is nipp'd, and ways be foul,
Then nightly sings the staring owl,
                              Tu-who;
To-whit, tu-who—a merry note,
While greasy Joan doth keel the pot.

IV

When all aloud the wind doth blow,
    And coughing drowns the parson's saw,
And birds sit brooding in the snow,
    And Marion's nose looks red and raw,
When roasted crabs hiss in the bowl,
Then nightly sings the staring owl,
                            Tu-who;
Tu-whit, tu-who—a merry note,
While greasy Joan doth keel the pot.

Now entertain conjecture of a time
When creeping murmur and the poring dark
Fills the wide vessel of the universe.
From camp to camp, through the foul womb of
    night,
The hum of either army stilly sounds,
That the fix'd sentinels almost receive
The secret whispers of each other's watch:
Fire answers fire, and through their paly flames
Each battle sees the other's umber'd face:
Steed threatens steed, in high and boastful neighs
Piercing the night's dull ear; and from the tents
The armourers, accomplishing the knights,
With busy hammers closing rivets up,
Give dreadful note of preparation.
The country cocks do crow, the clocks do toll,
And the third hour of drowsy morning name,

Proud of their numbers, and secure in soul,
The confident and over-lusty French
Do the low-rated English play at dice;
And chide the cripple tardy-gaited night
Who, like a foul and ugly witch, doth limp
So tediously away. The poor condemned English,
Like sacrifices, by their watchful fires
Sit patiently, and inly ruminate
The morning's danger, and their gesture sad
Investing lank-lean cheeks and war-worn coats
Presenteth them unto the gazing moon
So many horrid ghosts. O! now, who will behold
The royal captain of this ruin'd band
Walking from watch to watch, from tent to tent,
Let him cry "Praise and glory on his head!"
For forth he goes and visits all his host,
Bids them good morrow with a modest smile,
And calls them brothers, friends, and countrymen.
Upon his royal face there is no note
How dread an army hath enrounded him;
Nor doth he dedicate one jot of colour
Unto the weary and all-watched night:
But freshly looks and overbears attaint
With cheerful semblance and sweet majesty;
That every wretch, pining and pale before,
Beholding him, plucks comfort from his looks.
A largess universal, like the sun
His liberal eye doth give to every one,
Thawing cold fear. Then mean and gentle all,
Behold, as may unworthiness define,

A little touch of Harry in the night.
And so our scene must to the battle fly;
Where, — O for pity, — we shall much disgrace,
With four or five most vile and ragged foils,
Right ill dispos'd in brawl ridiculous,
The name of Agincourt.

                    All the world's a stage,
And all the men and women merely players:
They have their exits and their entrances;
And one man in his time plays many parts,
His acts being seven ages. At first the infant,
Mewling and puking in the nurse's arms.
And then the whining school-boy, with his satchel,
And shining morning face, creeping like snail
Unwilling to school. And then the lover,
Sighing like furnace, with a woeful ballad
Made to his mistress' eyebrow. Then a soldier,
Full of strange oaths, and bearded like the pard,
Jealous in honour, sudden and quick in quarrel,
Seeking the bubble reputation
Even in the cannon's mouth. And then the justice,
In fair round belly with good capon lin'd,
With eyes severe, and beard of formal cut,
Full of wise saws and modern instances;
And so he plays his part. The sixth age shifts
Into the lean and slipper'd pantaloon,
With spectacles on nose and pouch on side,

His youthful hose well sav'd, a world too wide
For his shrunk shank; and his big manly voice,
Turning again toward childish treble, pipes
And whistles in his sound. Last scene of all,
That ends this strange eventful history,
Is second childishness and mere oblivion,
Sans teeth, sans eyes, sans taste, sans everything.

Upon the king! let us our lives, our souls,
Our debts, our careful wives,
Our children, and our sins lay on the king!
We must bear all. O hard condition!
Twin-born with greatness, subject to the breath
Of every fool, whose sense no more can feel
But his own wringing. What infinite heart's ease
Must kings neglect that private men enjoy!
And what have kings that privates have not too,
Save ceremony, save general ceremony?
And what art thou, thou idle ceremony?
What kind of god art thou, that suffer'st more
Of mortal griefs than do thy worshippers?
What are thy rents? what are thy comings-in?
O ceremony! show me but thy worth.
What is thy soul of adoration?
Art thou aught else but place, degree, and form,
Creating awe and fear in other men?
Wherein thou art less happy, being fear'd,
Than they in fearing.

What drink'st thou oft, instead of homage sweet,
But poison'd flattery? O! be sick, great greatness,
And bid thy ceremony give thee cure.
Think'st thou the fiery fever will go out
With titles blown from adulation?
Will it give place to flexure and low-bending?
Canst thou, when thou command'st the beggar's
 knee,
Command the health of it? No, thou proud dream,
That play'st so subtly with a king's repose;
I am a king that find thee; and I know
'Tis not the balm, the sceptre and the ball,
The sword, the mace, the crown imperial,
The intertissued robe of gold and pearl,
The farced title running 'fore the king,
The throne he sits on, nor the tide of pomp
That beats upon the high shore of this world,
No, not all these, thrice-gorgeous ceremony,
Not all these, laid in bed majestical,
Can sleep so soundly as the wretched slave,
Who with a body fill'd and vacant mind
Gets him to rest, cramm'd with distressful bread;
Never sees horrid night, the child of hell,
But, like a lackey, from the rise to set
Sweats in the eye of Phœbus, and all night
Sleeps in Elysium; next day after dawn,
Doth rise and help Hyperion to his horse,
And follows so the ever-running year
With profitable labour to his grave:
And, but for ceremony, such a wretch,

Winding up days with toil and nights with sleep,
Had the fore-hand and vantage of a king.
The slave, a member of the country's peace,
Enjoys it; but in gross brain little wots
What watch the king keeps to maintain the peace,
Whose hours the peasant best advantages.

Once more unto the breach, dear friends, once
    more;
Or close the wall up with our English dead!
In peace there's nothing so becomes a man
As modest stillness and humility:
But when the blast of war blows in our ears,
Then imitate the action of the tiger;
Stiffen the sinews, summon up the blood,
Disguise fair nature with hard-favour'd rage;
Then lend the eye a terrible aspect;
Let it pry through the portage of the head
Like the brass cannon; let the brow o'erwhelm it
As fearfully as doth a galled rock
O'erhang and jutty his confounded base,
Swill'd with the wild and wasteful ocean.
Now set the teeth and stretch the nostril wide,
Hold hard the breath, and bend up every spirit
To his full height! On, on, you noblest English!
Whose blood is fet from fathers of war-proof;
Fathers that, like so many Alexanders,
Have in these parts from morn till even fought,

And sheath'd their swords for lack of argument.
Dishonour not your mothers; now attest
That those whom you call'd fathers did beget you.
Be copy now to men of grosser blood,
And teach them how to war. And you, good yeomen,
Whose limbs were made in England, show us here
The mettle of your pasture; let us swear
That you are worth your breeding; which I
    doubt not;
For there is none of you so mean and base
That hath not noble lustre in your eyes.
I see you stand like greyhounds in the slips,
Straining upon the start. The game's afoot:
Follow your spirit; and, upon this charge
Cry "God for Harry! England and Saint George!"

Let me not to the marriage of true minds
Admit impediments. Love is not love
Which alters when it alteration finds,
Or bends with the remover to remove:
O, no! it is an ever-fixed mark,
That looks on tempests and is never shaken;
It is the star to every wandering bark,
Whose worth's unknown, although his height be
    taken.
Love's not Time's fool, though rosy lips and cheeks
Within his bending sickle's compass come;
Love alters not with his brief hours and weeks,

But bears it out even to the edge of doom.
　　If this be error, and upon me prov'd,
　　I never writ, nor no man ever lov'd.

—I did dislike the cut of a certain courtier's beard: he sent me word, if I said his beard was not cut well, he was in the mind it was: this is called the Retort Courteous. if I sent him word again, it was not well cut, he would send me word, he cut it to please himself: this is called the Quip Modest. If again, it was not well cut, he disabled my judgment: this is called the Reply Churlish. If again, it was not well cut, he would answer, I spake not true: this is called the Reproof Valiant: if again, it was not well cut, he would say, I lie: this is called the Countercheck Quarrelsome: and so to the Lie Circumstantial, and the Lie Direct.

—And how oft did you say his beard was not well cut?

—I durst go no further than the Lie Circumstantial, nor he durst not give me the Lie Direct; and so we measured swords and parted.

—Can you nominate in order now the degrees of the lie?

—O sir, we quarrel in print; by the book, as you have books for good manners: I will name you the degrees. The first, the Retort Courteous; the second, the Quip Modest; the third, the Reply Churlish; the fourth, the Reproof Valiant; the fifth, the Countercheck Quarrelsome; the sixth, the Lie with Circumstance; the seventh, the Lie Direct. All these you may avoid but the Lie Direct; and you may avoid that too, with an "if." I knew when seven justices could not take up a quarrel; but when the parties were met themselves, one of them thought but of an "if," as "If you said so, then I said so;" and they shook hands and swore brothers. Your "if" is the only peace-maker; much virtue in "if."

Not mine own fears, nor the prophetic soul
Of the wide world dreaming on things to come,
Can yet the lease of my true love control,
Suppos'd as forfeit to a confin'd doom.
The mortal moon hath her eclipse endur'd,
And the sad augurs mock their own presage;
Incertainties now crown themselves assur'd,
And peace proclaims olives of endless age.
Now with the drops of this most balmy time
My love looks fresh, and Death to me subscribes,
Since, spite of him, I'll live in this poor rime,
While he insults o'er dull and speechless tribes:
    And thou in this shalt find thy monument,
    When tyrants' crests and tombs of brass are
    spent.

O! pardon me, thou bleeding piece of earth,
That I am meek and gentle with these butchers;
Thou art the ruins of the noblest man

That ever lived in the tide of times.
Woe to the hand that shed this costly blood!
Over thy wounds now do I prophesy,
Which like dumb mouths do ope their ruby lips,
To beg the voice and utterance of my tongue,
A curse shall light upon the limbs of men;
Domestic fury and fierce civil strife
Shall cumber all the parts of Italy;
Blood and destruction shall be so in use,
And dreadful objects so familiar,
That mothers shall but smile when they behold
Their infants quarter'd with the hands of war;
All pity chok'd with custom of fell deeds:
And Cæsar's spirit, ranging for revenge,
With Ate by his side come hot from hell,
Shall in these confines with a monarch's voice
Cry "Havoc!" and let slip the dogs of war;
That this foul deed shall smell above the earth
With carrion men, groaning for burial.

Were't aught to me I bore the canopy,
With my extern the outward honouring,
Or laid great bases for eternity,
Which prove more short than waste or ruining?
Have I not seen dwellers on form and favour
Lose all and more by paying too much rent,
For compound sweet foregoing simple savour

Pitiful thrivers, in their gazing spent?
No; let me be obsequious in thy heart,
And take thou my oblation, poor but free,
Which is not mix'd with seconds, knows no art,
But mutual render, only me for thee.
    Hence, thou suborn'd informer! a true soul
    When most impeach'd stands least in thy control.

If we are mark'd to die, we are enow
To do our country loss; and if to live,
The fewer men, the greater share of honour.
God's will! I pray thee, wish not one man more.
By Jove, I am not covetous for gold,
Nor care I who doth feed upon my cost;
It yearns me not if men my garments wear;
Such outward things dwell not in my desires:
But if it be a sin to covet honour,
I am the most offending soul alive.
No, faith, my coz, wish not a man from England:
God's peace! I would not lose so great an honour
As one man more, methinks, would shake from me,
For the best hope I have. O! do not wish one more:
Rather proclaim it, Westmoreland, through my host,
That he which hath no stomach to this fight,
Let him depart: his passport shall be made,
And crowns for convoy put into his purse:
We would not die in that man's company

That fears his fellowship to die with us.
This day is call'd the feast of Crispian:
He that outlives this day, and comes safe home,
Will stand a tip-toe when this day is nam'd,
And rouse him at the name of Crispian.
He that shall live this day, and see old age,
Will yearly on the vigil feast his neighbours,
And say, "To-morrow is Saint Crispian":
Then will he strip his sleeve and show his scars,
And say, "These wounds I had on Crispin's day."
Old men forget: yet all shall be forgot,
But he'll remember with advantages
What feats he did that day. Then shall our names,
Familiar in his mouth as household words,
Harry the king, Bedford and Exeter,
Warwick and Talbot, Salisbury and Gloucester,
Be in their flowing cups freshly remember'd.
This story shall the good man teach his son;
And Crispin Crispian shall ne'er go by,
From this day to the ending of the world,
But we in it shall be remembered;
We few, we happy few, we band of brothers;
For he to-day that sheds his blood with me
Shall be my brother; be he ne'er so vile
This day shall gentle his condition:
And gentlemen in England now a-bed
Shall think themselves accurs'd they were not here,
And hold their manhoods cheap whiles any speaks
That fought with us upon Saint Crispin's day.

—Even or odd of all days in the year,
Come Lammas-eve at night shall she be fourteen.
Susan and she—God rest all Christian souls!—
Were of an age. Well, Susan is with God;
She was too good for me. But, as I said,
On Lammas-eve at night shall she be fourteen;
That shall she, marry; I remember it well.
'Tis since the earthquake now eleven years;
And she was wean'd, I never shall forget it,
Of all the days of the year, upon that day;
For I had then laid wormwood to my dug,
Sitting in the sun under the dove-house wall;
My lord and you were then at Mantua.
Nay, I do bear a brain:—but, as I said,
When it did taste the wormwood on the nipple
Of my dug and felt it bitter, pretty fool!
To see it tetchy and fall out with the dug.
"Shake," quoth the dove-house: 'twas no need, I
    trow
To bid me trudge:
And since that time it is eleven years;
For then she could stand high lone; nay, by the
    rood,
She could have run and waddled all about;
For even the day before she broke her brow:
And then my husband—God be with his soul!
A' was a merry man—took up the child:
"Yea," quoth he, "dost thou fall upon thy face?
Thou wilt fall backward when thou hast more wit;
Wilt thou not, Jule?" and, by my halidom,

The pretty wretch left crying, and said "Ay."
To see now how a jest shall come about!
I warrant, an I should live a thousand years,
I never should forget it: "Wilt thou not, Jule?"
    quoth he;
And, pretty fool, it stinted and said "Ay."
    —Enough of this; I pray thee, hold thy peace.
    —Yes, madam. Yet I cannot choose but laugh,
To think it should leave crying, and say "Ay."
And yet, I warrant, it had upon its brow
A bump as big as a young cockerel's stone;
A parlous knock; and it cried bitterly:
"Yea," quoth my husband, "fall'st upon thy face?
Thou wilt fall backward when thou com'st to age;
Wilt thou not, Jule?" it stinted and said "Ay."

'Tis better to be vile than vile esteem'd,
When not to be receives reproach of being;
And the just pleasure lost, which is so deem'd
Not by our feeling, but by others' seeing:
For why should others' false adulterate eyes
Give salutation to my sportive blood?
Or on my frailties why are frailer spies,
Which in their wills count bad what I think good?
No, I am that I am, and they that level
At my abuses reckon up their own:
I may be straight though they themselves be
    bevel;

By their rank thoughts my deeds must not be
    shown;
        Unless this general evil they maintain,
        All men are bad and in their badness reign.

The quality of mercy is not strain'd,
It droppeth as the gentle rain from heaven
Upon the place beneath: it is twice bless'd;
It blesseth him that gives and him that takes:
'Tis mightiest in the mightiest; it becomes
The throned monarch better than his crown;
His sceptre shows the force of temporal power,
The attribute to awe and majesty,
Wherein doth sit the dread and fear of kings;
But mercy is above this sceptred sway,
It is enthroned in the hearts of kings,
It is an attribute to God himself,
        And earthly power doth then show likest God's
        When mercy seasons justice.

Poor soul, the centre of my sinful earth,
Fool'd by these rebel powers that thee array,
Why dost thou pine within and suffer dearth,
Painting thy outward walls so costly gay?
Why so large cost, having so short a lease,
Dost thou upon thy fading mansion spend?

Shall worms, inheritors of this excess,
Eat up thy charge? Is this thy body's end?
Then, soul, live thou upon thy servant's loss,
And let that pine to aggravate thy store;
Buy terms divine in selling hours of dross;
Within be fed, without be rich no more:
    So shalt thou feed on Death, that feeds on men,
    And Death once dead, there's no more dying
    then.

                        Of comfort no man speak:
Let's talk of graves, of worms, and epitaphs;
Make dust our paper, and with rainy eyes
Write sorrow on the bosom of the earth,
Let's choose executors and talk of wills:
And yet not so — for what can we bequeath
Save our deposed bodies to the ground?
Our lands, our lives, and all are Bolingbroke's,
And nothing can we call our own but death,
And that small model of the barren earth
Which serves as paste and cover to our bones.
For God's sake, let us sit upon the ground
And tell sad stories of the death of kings:
How some have been depos'd, some slain in war,
Some haunted by the ghosts they have depos'd,
Some poison'd by their wives, some sleeping kill'd;
All murder'd: for within the hollow crown
That rounds the mortal temples of a king

Keeps Death his court, and there the antick sits,
Scoffing his state and grinning at his pomp;
Allowing him a breath, a little scene,
To monarchize, be fear'd, and kill with looks,
Infusing him with self and vain conceit
As if this flesh which walls about our life
Were brass impregnable; and humour'd thus
Comes at the last, and with a little pin
Bores through his castle wall, and farewell king!
Cover your heads, and mock not flesh and blood
With solemn reverence: throw away respect,
Tradition, form, and ceremonious duty,
For you have but mistook me all this while:
I live with bread like you, feel want,
Taste grief, need friends: subjected thus,
How can you say to me I am a king?

Thine eyes I love, and they, as pitying me,
Knowing thy heart torments me with disdain,
Have put on black and loving mourners be,
Looking with pretty ruth upon my pain.
And truly not the morning sun of heaven
Better becomes the grey cheeks of the east,
Nor that full star that ushers in the even,
Doth half that glory to the sober west,
As those two mourning eyes become thy face.
O! let it then as well beseem thy heart
To mourn for me, since mourning doth thee grace,

And suit thy pity like in every part.
    Then will I swear beauty herself is black,
    And all they foul that thy complexion lack.

I do see the bottom of Justice Shallow. Lord, Lord! how subject we old men are to this vice of lying. This same starved justice hath done nothing but prate to me of the wildness of his youth and the feats he hath done about Turnbull Street; and every third word a lie, duer paid to the hearer than the Turk's tribute. I do remember him at Clement's Inn like a man made after supper of a cheese-paring: when a' was naked he was for all the world like a forked radish, with a head fantastically carved upon it with a knife: a' was so forlorn that his dimensions to any thick sight were invincible: a' was the very genius of famine; yet lecherous as a monkey, and the whores called him mandrake: a' came ever in the rearward of the fashion and sung those tunes to the overscutched huswives that he heard the carmen whistle, and sware they were his fancies or his good-nights. And now is this Vice's dagger become a squire, and talks as familiarly of John a Gaunt as if he had been sworn brother to him; and I'll be sworn a' never saw him but once in the Tilt-yard, and then he burst his head for crowding among the marshal's men. I saw it and told John a Gaunt he beat his own name; for you might have thrust him and all his apparel into an eel-skin; the case of a treble hautboy was a mansion for him, a court; and now has he land and beefs.

My mistress' eyes are nothing like the sun;
Coral is far more red than her lips' red;
If snow be white, why then her breasts are dun;
If hairs be wires, black wires grow on her head.
I have seen roses damask'd, red and white,
But no such roses see I in her cheeks;
And in some perfumes is there more delight
Than in the breath that from my mistress reeks.
I love to hear her speak, yet well I know
That music hath a far more pleasing sound:
I grant I never saw a goddess go, —
My mistress, when she walks, treads on the ground:
　　And yet, by heaven, I think my love as rare
　　As any she belied with false compare.

Grant them remov'd, and grant that this your noise
Hath chid down all the majesty of England;
Imagine that you see the wretched strangers,
Their babies at their backs, with their poor luggage,
Plodding to th' ports and coasts for transportation,
And that you sit as kings in your desires,
Authority quite silenc'd by your brawl,
And you in ruff of your opinions clothed,
What had you got? I'll tell you. You had taught
How insolence and strong hand should prevail,
How order should be quell'd — and by this pattern
Not one of you should live an aged man;

For other ruffians, as their fancies wrought,
With selfsame hand, self reasons and self right
Would shark on you, and men like ravenous fishes
Would feed on one another.
You'll put down strangers,
Kill them, cut their throats, possess their houses,
And lead the majesty of law in liom
To slip him like a hound. Say now the king
(As he is clement, if th' offender mourn)
Should so much come too short of your great
    trespass
As but to banish you—whither would you go?
What country, by the nature of your error,
Should give you harbour? Go you to France or
    Flanders,
To any German prince, to Spain or Portugal,
Nay, anywhere that not adheres to England,
Why, you must needs be strangers. Would you be
    pleas'd
To find a nation of such barbarous temper
That, breaking out in hideous violence,
Would not afford you an abode on earth,
Whet their detested knives against your throats,
Spurn you like dogs, and like as if that God
Ow'd not nor made not you, nor that the elements
Were not all appropriate to your comforts,
But charter'd unto them—what would you think
To be thus us'd? This is the strangers' case,
And this your mountainish inhumanity.

No longer mourn for me when I am dead
Than you shall hear the surly sullen bell
Give warning to the world that I am fled
From this vile world, with vilest worms to dwell:
Nay, if you read this line, remember not
The hand that writ it; for I love you so,
That I in your sweet thoughts would be forgot,
If thinking on me then should make you woe.
O! if, — I say, you look upon this verse,
When I perhaps compounded am with clay,
Do not so much as my poor name rehearse,
But let your love even with my life decay;
    Lest the wise world should look into your moan,
    And mock you with me after I am gone.

No, not an oath: if not the face of men,
The sufferance of our souls, the time's abuse,
If these be motives weak, break off betimes,
And every man hence to his idle bed;
So let high-sighted tyranny range on,
Till each man drop by lottery. But if these,
As I am sure they do, bear fire enough
To kindle cowards and to steel with valour
The melting spirits of women, then, countrymen,
What need we any spur but our own cause
To prick us to redress? what other bond
Than secret Romans, that have spoke the word

And will not palter? and what other oath
Than honesty to honesty engag'd,
That this shall be, or we will fall for it?
Swear priests and cowards and men cautelous,
Old feeble carrions and such suffering souls
That welcome wrongs; unto bad causes swear
Such creatures as men doubt; but do not stain
The even virtue of our enterprise,
Nor th' insuppressive mettle of our spirits,
To think that or our cause or our performance
Did need an oath; when every drop of blood
That every Roman bears, and nobly bears,
Is guilty of a several bastardy,
If he do break the smallest particle
Of any promise that hath pass'd from him.

The expense of spirit in a waste of shame
Is lust in action; and till action, lust
Is perjur'd, murderous, bloody, full of blame,
Savage, extreme, rude, cruel, not to trust;
Enjoy'd no sooner but despised straight;
Past reason hunted; and no sooner had,
Past reason hated, as a swallow'd bait,
On purpose laid to make the taker mad:
Mad in pursuit, and in possession so;
Had, having, and in quest to have, extreme;
A bliss in proof,—and prov'd, a very woe;

Before, a joy propos'd; behind, a dream.
  All this the world well knows; yet none knows well
  To shun the heaven that leads men to this hell.

Friends, Romans, countrymen, lend me your ears;
I come to bury Cæsar, not to praise him.
The evil that men do lives after them,
The good is oft interred with their bones;
So let it be with Cæsar. The noble Brutus
Hath told you Cæsar was ambitious;
If it were so, it was a grievous fault,
And grievously hath Cæsar answered it.
Here, under leave of Brutus and the rest,—
For Brutus is an honourable man;
So are they all, all honourable men,—
Come I to speak in Cæsar's funeral.
He was my friend, faithful and just to me:
But Brutus says he was ambitious;
And Brutus is an honourable man.
He hath brought many captives home to Rome,
Whose ransoms did the general coffers fill:
Did this in Cæsar seem ambitious?
When that the poor have cried, Cæsar hath wept;
Ambition should be made of sterner stuff:
Yet Brutus says he was ambitious;
And Brutus is an honourable man.
You all did see that on the Lupercal

I thrice presented him a kingly crown,
Which he did thrice refuse: was this ambition?
Yet Brutus says he was ambitious;
And, sure, he is an honourable man.
I speak not to disprove what Brutus spoke,
But here I am to speak what I do know.
You all did love him once, not without cause:
What cause withholds you then to mourn for him?
O judgment! thou art fled to brutish beasts,
And men have lost their reason. Bear with me;
My heart is in the coffin there with Cæsar,
And I must pause till it come back to me.

In faith, I do not love thee with mine eyes,
For they in thee a thousand errors note;
But 'tis my heart that loves what they despise,
Who, in despite of view, is pleas'd to dote.
Nor are mine ears with thy tongue's tune delighted;
Nor tender feeling, to base touches prone.
Nor taste nor smell desire to be invited
To any sensual feast with thee alone:
But my five wits nor my five senses can
Dissuade one foolish heart from serving thee,
Who leaves unsway'd the likeness of a man,
Thy proud heart's slave and vassal wretch to be:
    Only my plague thus far I count my gain,
    That she that makes me sin awards me pain.

Nay, you shall hear, Master Brook, what I have suffered to bring this woman to evil for your good. Being thus crammed in the basket, a couple of Ford's knaves, his hinds, were called forth by their mistress to carry me in the name of foul clothes to Datchet-lane: they took me on their shoulders; met the jealous knave their master in the door, who asked them once or twice what they had in their basket. I quaked for fear lest the lunatic knave would have searched it; but Fate, ordaining he should be a cuckold, held his hand. Well; on went he for a search, and away went I for foul clothes. But mark the sequel, Master Brook: I suffered the pangs of three several deaths: first, an intolerable fright, to be detected with a jealous rotten bell-wether; next, to be compassed, like a good bilbo, in the circumference of a peck, hilt to point, heel to head; and then, to be stopped in, like a strong distillation, with stinking clothes that fretted in their own grease: think of that, a man of my kidney, think of that, that am as subject to heat as butter; a man of continual dissolution and thaw: it was a miracle to 'scape suffocation. And in the height of this bath, when I was more than half stewed in grease, like a Dutch dish, to be thrown into the Thames, and cooled, glowing hot, in that surge, like a horse-shoe; think of that, hissing hot, think of that, Master Brook!

Two loves I have of comfort and despair,
Which like two spirits do suggest me still:

The better angel is a man right fair,
The worser spirit a woman, colour'd ill.
To win me soon to hell, my female evil
Tempteth my better angel from my side,
And would corrupt my saint to be a devil,
Wooing his purity with her foul pride.
And whether that my angel be turn'd fiend
Suspect I may, but not directly tell;
But being both from me, both to each friend,
I guess one angel in another's hell:
    Yet this shall I ne'er know, but live in doubt,
    Till my bad angel fire my good one out.

When that I was and a little tiny boy,
    With hey, ho, the wind and the rain;
A foolish thing was but a toy,
    For the rain it raineth every day.

But when I came to man's estate,
    With hey, ho, the wind and the rain;
'Gainst knaves and thieves men shut their
    gates,
    For the rain it raineth every day.

But when I came, alas! to wive,
    With hey, ho, the wind and the rain;
By swaggering could I never thrive,
    For the rain it raineth every day.

When my love swears that she is made of truth,
I do believe her, though I know she lies,
That she might think me some untutor'd youth,
Unlearned in the world's false subtleties.
Thus vainly thinking that she thinks me young,
Although she knows my days are past the best,
Simply I credit her false-speaking tongue:
On both sides thus is simple truth supprest.
But wherefore says she not she is unjust?
And wherefore say not I that I am old?
O! love's best habit is in seeming trust,
And age in love loves not to have years told:
    Therefore I lie with her, and she with me,
    And in our faults by lies we flatter'd be.

If I begin the battery once again,
I will not leave the half-achieved Harfleur
Till in her ashes she lie buried.
The gates of mercy shall be all shut up,
And the flesh'd soldier, rough and hard of heart,
In liberty of bloody hand shall range
With conscience wide as hell, mowing like grass
Your fresh-fair virgins and your flowering infants.
What is it then to me, if impious war,
Array'd in flames like to the prince of fiends,
Do, with his smirch'd complexion, all fell feats
Enlink'd to waste and desolation?
What is't to me, when you yourselves are cause,

If your pure maidens fall into the hand
Of hot and forcing violation?
What rein can hold licentious wickedness
When down the hill he holds his fierce career?
We may as bootless spend our vain command
Upon the enraged soldiers in their spoil
As send precepts to the leviathan
To come ashore. Therefore, you men of Harfleur,
Take pity of your town and of your people,
Whiles yet my soldiers are in my command;
Whiles yet the cool and temperate wind of grace
O'erblows the filthy and contagious clouds
Of heady murder, spoil, and villainy.
If not, why, in a moment, look to see
The blind and bloody soldier with foul hand
Defile the locks of your shrill-shrieking daughters;
Your fathers taken by the silver beards,
And their most reverend heads dash'd to the walls;
Your naked infants spitted upon pikes,
Whiles the mad mothers with their howls confus'd
Do break the clouds, as did the wives of Jewry
At Herod's bloody-hunting slaughtermen.
What say you? will you yield, and this avoid?

O me! what eyes hath Love put in my head,
Which have no correspondence with true sight;
Or, if they have, where is my judgment fled,
That censures falsely what they see aright?

If that be fair whereon my false eyes dote,
What means the world to say it is not so?
If it be not, then love doth well denote
Love's eye is not so true as all men's: no.
How can it? O! how can Love's eye be true,
That is so vex'd with watching and with tears
No marvel then, though I mistake my view;
The sun itself sees not till heaven clears.
　　O cunning Love! with tears thou keep'st me
　　blind,
　　　Lest eyes well-seeing thy foul faults should find.

Yon island carrions desperate of their bones,
Ill-favour'dly become the morning field;
Their ragged curtains poorly are let loose,
And our air shakes them passing scornfully:
Big Mars seems bankrupt in their beggar'd host,
And faintly through a rusty beaver peeps:
The horsemen sit like fixed candlesticks,
With torch-staves in their hand; and their poor
　　jades
Lob down their heads, dropping the hides and
　　hips,
The gum down-roping from their pale-dead eyes,
And in their pale dull mouths the gimmal bit
Lies foul with chew'd grass, still and motionless;
And their executors, the knavish crows,
Fly o'er them, all impatient for their hour.

My love is as a fever, longing still
For that which longer nurseth the disease;
Feeding on that which doth preserve the ill,
The uncertain sickly appetite to please.
My reason, the physician to my love,
Angry that his prescriptions are not kept,
Hath left me, and I desperate now approve
Desire is death, which physic did except.
Past cure I am, now Reason is past care,
And frantic mad with evermore unrest;
My thoughts and my discourse as madmen's are,
At random from the truth vainly express'd;
    For I have sworn thee fair, and thought thee
    bright,
    Who art as black as hell, as dark as night.

I think Crab my dog be the sourest natured dog
that lives: my mother weeping, my father wailing, my
sister crying, our maid howling, our cat wringing her
hands, and all our house in a great perplexity, yet
did not this cruel-hearted cur shed one tear. He is
a stone, a very pebble stone, and has no more pity
in him than a dog; a Jew would have wept to have
seen our parting: why, my grandam, having no eyes,
look you, wept herself blind at my parting. Nay, I'll
show you the manner of it. This shoe is my father;
no, this left shoe is my father: no, no, this left shoe
is my mother; nay, that cannot be so neither:—yes,
it is so; it is so; it hath the worser sole. This shoe,
with the hole in, is my mother, and this my father.

A vengeance on't! there 'tis: now, sir, this staff is my sister; for, look you, she is as white as a lily and as small as a wand: this hat is Nan, our maid: I am the dog; no, the dog is himself, and I am the dog,—O! the dog is me, and I am myself: ay, so, so. Now come I to my father; "Father, your blessing"; now should not the shoe speak a word for weeping: now should I kiss my father; well, he weeps on. Now come I to my mother;—O, that she could speak now like a wood woman! Well, I kiss her; why, there 'tis; here's my mother's breath up and down. Now come I to my sister; mark the moan she makes: Now the dog all this while sheds not a tear nor speaks a word; but see how I lay the dust with my tears.

Other slow arts entirely keep the brain,
And therefore, finding barren practisers,
Scarce show a harvest of their heavy toil;
But love, first learned in a lady's eyes,
Lives not alone immured in the brain,
But, with the motion of all elements,
Courses as swift as thought in every power,
And gives to every power a double power,
Above their functions and their offices.
It adds a precious seeing to the eye;
A lover's eyes will gaze an eagle blind;
A lover's ear will hear the lowest sound,
When the suspicious head of theft is stopp'd:
Love's feeling is more soft and sensible
Than are the tender horns of cockled snails:

Love's tongue proves dainty Bacchus gross in
    taste.
For valour, is not Love a Hercules,
Still climbing trees in the Hesperides?
Subtle as Sphinx; as sweet and musical
As bright Apollo's lute, strung with his hair;
And when Love speaks, the voice of all the gods
Makes heaven drowsy with the harmony.

She is the fairies' midwife, and she comes
In shape no bigger than an agate-stone
On the fore-finger of an alderman,
Drawn with a team of little atomies
Athwart men's noses as they lie asleep:
Her waggon-spokes made of long spinners' legs;
The cover, of the wings of grasshoppers;
The traces, of the smallest spider's web;
The collars, of the moonshine's watery beams;
Her whip, of cricket's bone; the lash, of film;
Her waggoner, a small grey-coated gnat,
Not half so big as a round little worm
Prick'd from the lazy finger of a maid;
Her chariot is an empty hazel-nut,
Made by the joiner squirrel or old grub,
Time out o' mind the fairies' coach-makers.
And in this state she gallops night by night
Through lovers' brains, and then they dream of
    love;

O'er courtiers' knees, that dream on curtsies
    straight;
O'er lawyers' fingers, who straight dream on fees;
O'er ladies' lips, who straight on kisses dream;
Which oft the angry Mab with blisters plagues,
Because their breaths with sweetmeats tainted are.
Sometimes she gallops o'er a courtier's nose,
And then dreams he of smelling out a suit;
And sometimes comes she with a tithe-pig's tail,
Tickling a parson's nose as a' lies asleep,
Then dreams he of another benefice;
Sometime she driveth o'er a soldier's neck,
And then dreams he of cutting foreign throats,
Of breaches, ambuscadoes, Spanish blades,
Of healths five fathom deep; and then anon
Drums in his ear, at which he starts and wakes;
And, being thus frighted, swears a prayer or two,
And sleeps again. This is that very Mab
That plats the manes of horses in the night;
And bakes the elf-locks in foul sluttish hairs,
Which once untangled much misfortune bodes;
This is the hag, when maids lie on their backs,
That presses them and learns them first to bear,
Making them women of good carriage:
This is she —

In loving thee thou know'st I am forsworn,
But thou art twice forsworn, to me love swearing;

In act thy bed-vow broke, and new faith torn,
In vowing new hate after new love bearing.
But why of two oaths' breach do I accuse thee,
When I break twenty? I am perjur'd most;
For all my vows are oaths but to misuse thee,
And all my honest faith in thee is lost:
For I have sworn deep oaths of thy deep
    kindness,
Oaths of thy love, thy truth, thy constancy;
And, to enlighten thee, gave eyes to blindness,
Or made them swear against the thing they see;
    For I have sworn thee fair; more perjur'd I,
    To swear against the truth so foul a lie!

I would I had that corporal soundness now,
As when thy father and myself in friendship
First tried our soldiership! He did look far
Into the service of the time and was
Discipled of the bravest: he lasted long,
But on us both did haggish age steal on,
And wore us out of act. It much repairs me
To talk of your good father. In his youth
He had the wit which I can well observe
To-day in our young lords; but they may jest
Till their own scorn return to them unnoted
Ere they can hide their levity in honour.
So like a courtier, contempt nor bitterness
Were in his pride or sharpness; if they were,

His equal had awak'd them; and his honour,
Clock to itself, knew the true minute when
Exception bid him speak, and at this time
His tongue obey'd his hand: who were below him
He us'd as creatures of another place,
And bow'd his eminent top to their low ranks,
Making them proud of his humility,
In their poor praise he humbled. Such a man
Might be a copy to these younger times,
Which, follow'd well, would demonstrate
     them now
But goers backward.
Would I were with him! He would always say,—
Methinks I hear him now: his plausive words
He scatter'd not in ears, but grafted them,
To grow there and to bear. "Let me not live,"—
Thus his good melancholy oft began,
On the catastrophe and heel of pastime,
When it was out,—"Let me not live," quoth he,
"After my flame lacks oil, to be the snuff
Of younger spirits, whose apprehensive senses
All but new things disdain; whose judgments are
Mere fathers of their garments; whose
     constancies
Expire before their fashions." This he wish'd:
I, after him, do after him wish too,
Since I nor wax nor honey can bring home,
I quickly were dissolved from my hive,
To give some labourers room.

And suddenly; where injury of chance
Puts back leave-taking, justles roughly by
All time of pause, rudely beguiles our lips
Of all rejoindure, forcibly prevents
Our lock'd embrasures, strangles our dear vows
Even in the birth of our own labouring breath.
We two, that with so many thousand sighs
Did buy each other, must poorly sell ourselves
With the rude brevity and discharge of one.
Injurious time now with a robber's haste
Crams his rich thievery up, he knows not how:
As many farewells as be stars in heaven,
With distinct breath and consign'd kisses to them,
He fumbles up into a loose adieu,
And scants us with a single famish'd kiss,
Distasted with the salt of broken tears.

                                    Fie, fie upon her!
There's language in her eye, her cheek, her lip,
Nay, her foot speaks; her wanton spirits look out
At every joint and motive of her body.
O! these encounters, so glib of tongue,
That give a coasting welcome ere it comes,
And wide unclasp the tables of their thoughts
To every tickling reader, set them down
For sluttish spoils of opportunity
And daughters of the game.

Be absolute for death; either death or life
Shall thereby be the sweeter. Reason thus with life:
If I do lose thee, I do lose a thing
That none but fools would keep: a breath thou art,
Servile to all the skyey influences,
That dost this habitation, where thou keep'st,
Hourly afflict. Merely, thou art death's fool;
For him thou labour'st by thy flight to shun,
And yet run'st toward him still. Thou art not noble;
For all th' accommodations that thou bear'st
Are nurs'd by baseness. Thou art by no means
    valiant;
For thou dost fear the soft and tender fork
Of a poor worm. Thy best of rest is sleep,
And that thou oft provok'st; yet grossly fear'st
Thy death, which is no more. Thou art not thyself;
For thou exist'st on many a thousand grains
That issue out of dust. Happy thou art not;
For what thou hast not, still thou striv'st to get,
And what thou hast, forget'st. Thou art not certain;
For thy complexion shifts to strange effects,
After the moon. If thou art rich, thou'rt poor;
For, like an ass whose back with ingots bows,
Thou bear'st thy heavy riches but a journey,
And death unloads thee. Friend hast thou none;
For thine own bowels, which do call thee sire,
The mere effusion of thy proper loins,
Do curse the gout, serpigo, and the rheum,
For ending thee no sooner. Thou hast nor youth
    nor age;

But, as it were, an after-dinner's sleep,
Dreaming on both; for all thy blessed youth
Becomes as aged, and doth beg the alms
Of palsied eld; and when thou art old and rich,
Thou hast neither heat, affection, limb, nor beauty,
To make thy riches pleasant. What's yet in this
That bears the name of life? Yet in this life
Lie hid moe thousand deaths: yet death we fear,
That makes these odds all even.

Come, how wouldst thou praise me?
    I am about it; but indeed my invention
    Comes from my pate as birdlime does from frize;
    It plucks out brains and all: but my muse labours,
    And thus she is deliver'd
    If she be fair and wise, fairness and wit,
    The one's for use, the other useth it.
Well prais'd! How if she be black and witty?
    If she be black, and thereto have a wit,
    She'll find a white that shall her blackness fit.
How if fair and foolish?
    She never yet was foolish that was fair,
    For even her folly help'd her to an heir.
*These are old fond paradoxes to make fools laugh i' the
alehouse. What miserable praise hast thou for her that's
foul and foolish?*
    There's none so foul and foolish thereunto
    But does foul pranks which fair and wise ones do.

O heavy ignorance! thou praisest the worst best. But what praise couldst thou bestow on a deserving woman indeed, one that in the authority of her merit, did justly put on the vouch of very malice itself?

> She that was ever fair and never proud,
> Had tongue at will and yet was never loud,
> Never lack'd gold and yet went never gay,
> Fled from her wish and yet said "Now I may,"
> She that being anger'd, her revenge being nigh,
> Bade her wrong stay and her displeasure fly,
> She that in wisdom never was so frail
> To change the cod's head for the salmon's tail,
> She that could think and ne'er disclose her
> mind.
> See suitors following and not look behind,
> She was a wight, if ever such wight were,—

To do what?

> To suckle fools and chronicle small beer.

O most lame and impotent conclusion! Do not learn of him.

I have of late,—but wherefore I know not,—lost all my mirth, forgone all custom of exercises; and indeed it goes so heavily with my disposition that this goodly frame, the earth, seems to me a sterile promontory; this most excellent canopy, the air, look you, this brave o'erhanging firmament, this majestical roof fretted with golden fire, why, it appears no other thing to me but a foul and pestilent congregation of vapours. What a piece of work is a man! How noble in reason! how infinite in faculty! in form, in moving, how express and admirable! in action how like an angel! in apprehension how like a god! the beauty of the world! the paragon of animals! And yet, to me, what is this quintessence of dust? man delights not me; no, nor woman neither, though, by your smiling, you seem to say so.

O! that I thought it could be in a woman—
As if it can I will presume in you—
To feed for aye her lamp and flames of love;
To keep her constancy in plight and youth,
Outliving beauty's outward, with a mind
That doth renew swifter than blood decays;
Or that persuasion could but thus convince me,
That my integrity and truth to you
Might be affronted with the match and weight
Of such a winnow'd purity in love;
How were I then uplifted! but, alas!
I am as true as truth's simplicity,
And simpler than the infancy of truth

—He eats nothing but doves, love; and that breeds hot blood, and hot blood begets hot thoughts, and hot thoughts beget hot deeds, and hot deeds is love.

—Is this the generation of love? hot blood? hot thoughts, and hot deeds? Why, they are vipers: is love a generation of vipers?

If I be false, or swerve a hair from truth,
When time is old and hath forgot itself,
When waterdrops have worn the stones of Troy,
And blind oblivion swallow'd cities up,
And mighty states characterless are grated
To dusty nothing, yet let memory,
From false to false, among false maids in love
Upbraid my falsehood! when they have said as false
As air, as water, wind, or sandy earth,
As fox to lamb, as wolf to heifer's calf,
Pard to the hind, or stepdame to her son;
Yea, let them say, to stick the heart of falsehood,
"As false as Cressid."

I follow him to serve my turn upon him;
We cannot all be masters, nor all masters
Cannot be truly follow'd. You shall mark
Many a duteous and knee-crooking knave,
That, doting on his own obsequious bondage,
Wears out his time, much like his master's ass,
For nought but provender, and when he's old,
    cashier'd;
Whip me such honest knaves. Others there are
Who, trimm'd in forms and visages of duty,
Keep yet their hearts attending on themselves,
And, throwing but shows of service on their lords,
Do well thrive by them, and when they have lin'd
    their coats

Do themselves homage: these fellows have some soul;
And such a one do I profess myself. For, sir,
It is as sure as you are Roderigo,
Were I the Moor, I would not be Iago:
In following him, I follow but myself;
Heaven is my judge, not I for love and duty,
But seeming so, for my peculiar end:
For when my outward action doth demonstrate
The native act and figure of my heart
In compliment extern, 'tis not long after
But I will wear my heart upon my sleeve
For daws to peck at: I am not what I am.

Aye, but to die, and go we know not where;
To lie in cold obstruction and to rot,
This sensible warm motion to become
A kneaded clod; and the delighted spirit
To bathe in fiery floods, or to reside
In thrilling region of thick-ribbed ice;
To be imprison'd in the viewless winds,
And blown with restless violence round about
The pendant world; or to be worse than worst
Of those that lawless and incertain thoughts
Imagine howling: 'tis too horrible!
The weariest and most loathed worldly life
That age, ache, penury and imprisonment
Can lay on nature is a paradise
To what we fear of death.

Take, O take those lips away,
   That so sweetly were forsworn;
And those eyes, the break of day,
   Lights that do mislead the morn:
But my kisses bring again,   bring again,
Seals of love, but seal'd in vain,   seal'd in vain.

But I do think it is their husbands' faults
If wives do fall. Say that they slack their duties,
And pour our treasures into foreign laps,
Or else break out in peevish jealousies,
Throwing restraint upon us; or, say they strike us,
Or scant our former having in despite;
Why, we have galls, and though we have some grace,
Yet have we some revenge. Let husbands know
Their wives have sense like them; they see and smell,
And have their palates both for sweet and sour,
As husbands have. What is it that they do
When they change us for others? Is it sport?
I think it is; and doth affection breed it?
I think it doth; is't frailty that thus errs?
It is so too; and have not we affections,
Desires for sport, and frailty, as men have?
Then, let them use us well; else let them know,
The ills we do, their ills instruct us so.

There, my blessing with thee!
And these few precepts in thy memory
Look thou character. Give thy thoughts no tongue,

Nor any unproportion'd thought his act.
Be thou familiar, but by no means vulgar;
The friends thou hast, and their adoption tried,
Grapple them to thy soul with hoops of steel;
But do not dull thy palm with entertainment
Of each new-hatch'd, unfledg'd comrade. Beware
Of entrance to a quarrel, but, being in,
Bear't that th' opposed may beware of thee.
Give every man thine ear, but few thy voice;
Take each man's censure, but reserve thy judgment.
Costly thy habit as thy purse can buy,
But not express'd in fancy; rich, not gaudy;
For the apparel oft proclaims the man,
And they in France of the best rank and station
Are most select and generous, chief in that.
Neither a borrower, nor a lender be;
For loan oft loses both itself and friend,
And borrowing dulls the edge of husbandry.
This above all: to thine own self be true,
And it must follow, as the night the day,
Thou canst not then be false to any man.
Farewell; my blessing season this in thee!

Had it pleas'd heaven
To try me with affliction, had he rain'd
All kinds of sores, and shames, on my bare head,
Steep'd me in poverty to the very lips,
Given to captivity me and my utmost hopes,

I should have found in some part of my soul
A drop of patience; but, alas! to make me
The fixed figure for the time of scorn
To point his slow and moving finger at;
Yet could I bear that too; well, very well.
But there, where I have garner'd up my heart,
Where either I must live or bear no life,
The fountain from the which my current runs
Or else dries up; to be discarded thence!
Or keep it as a cistern for foul toads
To knot and gender in!

O! beware, my lord, of jealousy;
It is the green-ey'd monster which doth mock
The meat it feeds on; that cuckold lives in bliss
Who, certain of his fate, loves not his wronger;
But, O! what damned minutes tells he o'er
Who dotes, yet doubts; suspects, yet strongly loves!
Poor and content is rich, and rich enough,
But riches fineless is as poor as winter.
To him that ever fears he shall be poor.
Good heaven, the souls of all my tribe defend
From jealousy!

O! that this too too solid flesh would melt,
Thaw, and resolve itself into a dew;

Or that the Everlasting had not fix'd
His canon 'gainst self-slaughter! O God! O God!
How weary, stale, flat, and unprofitable
Seem to me all the uses of this world.
Fie on't! O fie! 'tis an unweeded garden,
That grows to seed; things rank and gross in nature
Possess it merely. That it should come to this!
But two months dead: nay, not so much, not two:
So excellent a king; that was, to this,
Hyperion to a satyr; so loving to my mother
That he might not beteem the winds of heaven
Visit her face too roughly. Heaven and earth!
Must I remember? why, she would hang on him,
As if increase of appetite had grown
By what it fed on; and yet, within a month,
Let me not think on't: Frailty, thy name is woman!
A little month; or ere those shoes were old
With which she follow'd my poor father's body,
Like Niobe, all tears; why she, even she,—
O God! a beast, that wants discourse of reason,
Would have mourn'd longer,—married with mine
    uncle,
My father's brother, but no more like my father
Than I to Hercules: within a month,
Ere yet the salt of most unrighteous tears
Had left the flushing in her galled eyes,
She married. O! most wicked speed, to post
With such dexterity to incestuous sheets.
It is not nor it cannot come to good;
But break, my heart, for I must hold my tongue!

Who is Silvia? what is she,
    That all our swains commend her?
Holy, fair, and wise is she:
    The heaven such grace did lend her,
That she might admired be.

Is she kind as she is fair?
    For beauty lives with kindness:
Love doth to her eyes repair,
    To help him of his blindness;
And, being help'd, inhabits there.

Then to Silvia let us sing,
    That Silvia is excelling;
She excels each mortal thing
    Upon the dull earth dwelling;
To her let us garlands bring.

We have strict statutes and most biting laws,—
The needful bits and curbs to headstrong
    steeds,—
Which for this fourteen years we have let sleep;
Even like an o'ergrown lion in a cave,
That goes not out to prey. Now, as fond fathers,
Having bound up the threat'ning twigs of birch,
Only to stick it in their children's sight
For terror, not to use, in time the rod
Becomes more mock'd than fear'd; so our decrees,

Dead to infliction, to themselves are dead,
And liberty plucks justice by the nose;
The baby beats the nurse, and quite athwart
Goes all decorum.

Good name in man and woman, dear my lord,
Is the immediate jewel of their souls:
Who steals my purse steals trash; 'tis something,
    nothing;
'Twas mine, 'tis his, and has been slave to thousands;
But he that filches from me my good name
Robs me of that which not enriches him,
And makes me poor indeed.

Virtue! a fig! 'tis in ourselves that we are thus, or
thus. Our bodies are our gardens, to the which our
wills are gardeners; so that if we will plant nettles or
sow lettuce, set hyssop and weed up thyme, supply
it with one gender of herbs or distract it with many,
either to have it sterile with idleness or manured with
industry, why, the power and corrigible authority of
this lies in our wills. If the balance of our lives had
not one scale of reason to poise another of sensuality,
the blood and baseness of our natures would conduct
us to most preposterous conclusions; but we have
reason to cool our raging motions, our carnal stings,
our unbitted lusts, whereof I take this that you call
love to be a sect or scion.

O thou foul thief! where hast thou stow'd my
   daughter?
Damned as thou art, thou hast enchanted her;
For I'll refer me to all things of sense,
If she in chains of magic were not bound,
Whether a maid so tender, fair, and happy,
So opposite to marriage that she shunn'd
The wealthy curled darlings of our nation,
Would ever have, to incur a general mock,
Run from her guardage to the sooty bosom
Of such a thing as thou; to fear, not to delight.
Judge me the world, if 'tis not gross in sense
That thou hast practis'd on her with foul charms,
Abus'd her delicate youth with drugs or minerals
That weaken motion: I'll have't disputed on;
'Tis probable, and palpable to thinking.
I therefore apprehend and do attach thee
For an abuser of the world, a practiser
Of arts inhibited and out of warrant.
Lay hold upon him: if he do resist,
Subdue him at his peril.

O! what a rogue and peasant slave am I:
Is it not monstrous that this player here,
But in a fiction, in a dream of passion,
Could force his soul so to his own conceit
That from her working all his visage wann'd,
Tears in his eyes, distraction in's aspect,

A broken voice, and his whole function suiting
With forms to his conceit? and all for nothing!
For Hecuba!
What's Hecuba to him or he to Hecuba
That he should weep for her? What would he do
Had he the motive and the cue for passion
That I have? He would drown the stage with tears,
And cleave the general ear with horrid speech,
Make mad the guilty and appal the free,
Confound the ignorant, and amaze indeed
The very faculties of eyes and ears. Yet I,
A dull and muddy-mettled rascal, peak,
Like John-a-dreams, unpregnant of my cause,
And can say nothing; no, not for a king,
Upon whose property and most dear life
A damn'd defeat was made. Am I a coward?
Who calls me villain? breaks my pate across?
Plucks off my beard and blows it in my face?
Tweaks me by the nose? gives me the lie i' the
    throat,
As deep as to the lungs? Who does me this? Ha!
Swounds, I should take it, for it cannot be
But I am pigeon-liver'd, and lack gall
To make oppression bitter, or ere this
I should have fatted all the region kites
With this slave's offal. Bloody, bawdy villain!
Remorseless, treacherous, lecherous, kindless
    villain!
O! vengeance!
Why, what an ass am I! This is most brave

That I, the son of a dear father murder'd,
Prompted to my revenge by heaven and hell,
Must, like a whore, unpack my heart with words,
And fall a-cursing, like a very drab,
A scullion! Fie upon't! foh! About, my brain!

                              If I do prove her haggard
Though that her jesses were my dear heart-strings,
I'd whistle her off and let her down the wind,
To prey at fortune. Haply, for I am black,
And have not those soft parts of conversation
That chamberers have, or, for I am declin'd
Into the vale of years—yet that's not much—
She's gone, I am abus'd; and my relief
Must be to loathe her. O curse of marriage!
That we can call these delicate creatures ours,
And not their appetites. I had rather be a toad,
And live upon the vapour of a dungeon,
Than keep a corner in the thing I love
For others' uses. Yet, 'tis the plague of great ones;
Prerogativ'd are they less than the base;
'Tis destiny unshunnable, like death:
Even then this forked plague is fated to us
When we do quicken.

Degree being vizarded,
The unworthiest shows as fairly in the mask.

The heavens themselves, the planets, and this centre
Observe degree, priority, and place,
Insisture, course, proportion, season, form,
Office, and custom, in all line of order:
And therefore is the glorious planet Sol
In noble eminence enthron'd and spher'd
Amidst the other; whose med'cinable eye
Corrects the ill aspects of planets evil,
And posts, like the commandment of a king,
Sans check, to good and bad: but when the planets
In evil mixture to disorder wander,
What plagues, and what portents, what mutiny,
What raging of the sea, shaking of earth,
Commotion in the winds, frights, changes, horrors,
Divert and crack, rend and deracinate
The unity and married calm of states
Quite from their fixture! O! when degree is shak'd.
Which is the ladder to all high designs,
The enterprise is sick. How could communities,
Degrees in schools, and brotherhoods in cities,
Peaceful commerce from dividable shores,
The primogenitive and due of birth,
Prerogative of age, crowns, sceptres, laurels,
But by degree, stand in authentic place?
Take but degree away, untune that string,
And, hark! what discord follows; each thing meets
In mere oppugnancy: the bounded waters
Should lift their bosoms higher than the shores,
And make a sop of all this solid globe:
Strength should be lord of imbecility,

And the rude son should strike his father dead:
Force should be right; or rather, right and
   wrong—
Between whose endless jar justice resides—
Should lose their names, and so should justice too.
Then every thing includes itself in power,
Power into will, will into appetite;
And appetite, a universal wolf,
So doubly seconded with will and power,
Must make perforce a universal prey,
And last eat up himself.

I am giddy, expectation whirls me round.
The imaginary relish is so sweet
That it enchants my sense. What will it be
When that the watery palate tastes indeed
Love's thrice-repured nectar? death, I fear me,
Swounding destruction, or some joy too fine,
Too subtle-potent, tun'd too sharp in sweetness
For the capacity of my ruder powers:
I fear it much; and I do fear besides
That I shall lose distinction in my joys;
As doth a battle, when they charge on heaps
The enemy flying.

   —Lay thy finger thus, and let thy soul be instructed.
Mark me with what violence she first loved the Moor
but for bragging and telling her fantastical lies; and

will she love him still for prating? let not thy discreet heart think it. Her eye must be fed; and what delight shall she have to look on the devil? When the blood is made dull with the act of sport, there should be, again to inflame it, and to give satiety a fresh appetite, loveliness in favour, sympathy in years, manners, and beauties; all which the Moor is defective in. Now, for want of these required conveniences, her delicate tenderness will find itself abused, begin to heave the gorge, disrelish and abhor the Moor; very nature will instruct her in it, and compel her to some second choice. Now, sir, this granted, as it is a most pregnant and unforced position, who stands so eminently in the degree of this fortune as Cassio does? a knave very voluble, no further conscionable than in putting on the mere form of civil and humane seeming, for the better compassing of his salt and most hidden loose affection? why, none; why, none; a slipper and subtle knave, a finder-out of occasions, that has an eye can stamp and counterfeit advantages, though true advantage never present itself; a devilish knave! Besides, the knave is handsome, young, and hath all those requisites in him that folly and green minds look after; a pestilent complete knave! and the woman hath found him already.

—I cannot believe that in her; she is full of most blessed condition.

—Blessed fig's end! the wine she drinks is made of grapes; if she had been blessed she would never have loved the Moor; blessed pudding! Didst thou not see her paddle with the palm of his hand? didst not mark that?

—Yes, that I did; but that was but courtesy.

—Lechery, by this hand! an index and obscure prologue to the history of lust and foul thoughts. They met so near with their lips, that their breaths embraced together. Villainous thoughts, Roderigo! when these mutualities so marshal the way, hard at hand comes the master and main exercise, the incorporate conclusion. Pish!

—Renew, renew! The fierce Polydamas
Hath beat down Menon; bastard Margarelon
Hath Doreus prisoner,
And stands colossus-wise, waving his beam,
Upon the pashed corses of the kings
Epistrophus and Cedius; Polixenes is slain;
Amphimachus, and Thoas, deadly hurt;
Patroclus ta'en, or slain; and Palamedes
Sore hurt and bruis'd; the dreadful Sagittary
Appals our numbers: haste we, Diomed,
To reinforcement, or we perish all.

—Go, bear Patroclus' body to Achilles;
And bid the snail-pac'd Ajax arm for shame.
There is a thousand Hectors in the field:
Now here he fights on Galathe his horse,
And there lacks work; anon he's there afoot,
And there they fly or die, like scaled sculls
Before the belching whale; then is he yonder,
And there the strawy Greeks, ripe for his edge,

Fall down before him, like the mower's swath:
Here, there, and everywhere, he leaves and takes,
Dexterity so obeying appetite
That what he will he does; and does so much
That proof is called impossibility.
    —O! courage, courage, princes; great Achilles
Is arming, weeping, cursing, vowing vengeance:
Patroclus' wounds have rous'd his drowsy blood,
Together with his mangled Myrmidons,
That noseless, handless, hack'd and chipp'd, come
    to him,
Crying on Hector. Ajax hath lost a friend,
And foams at mouth, and he is arm'd and at it,
Roaring for Troilus, who hath done to-day
Mad and fantastic execution,
Engaging and redeeming of himself
With such a careless force and forceless care
As if that luck, in very spite of cunning,
Bade him win all.

Get thee to a nunnery: why wouldst thou be a
breeder of sinners? I am myself indifferent honest;
but yet I could accuse me of such things that it were
better my mother had not borne me. I am very proud,
revengeful, ambitious; with more offences at my beck
than I have thoughts to put them in, imagination to
give them shape, or time to act them in. What should
such fellows as I do crawling between heaven and
earth? We are arrant knaves, all; believe none of us.
Go thy ways to a nunnery....

If thou dost marry, I'll give thee this plague for thy dowry: be thou as chaste as ice, as pure as snow, thou shalt not escape calumny. Get thee to a nunnery, go; farewell. Or, if thou wilt needs marry, marry a fool; for wise men know well enough what monsters you make of them. To a nunnery, go; and quickly too. Farewell.

I have heard of your paintings too, well enough; God hath given you one face, and you make yourselves another: you jig, you amble, and you lisp, and nickname God's creatures, and make your wantonness your ignorance. Go to, I'll no more on't; it hath made me mad. I say, we will have no more marriages; those that are married already, all but one, shall live; the rest shall keep as they are. To a nunnery, go.

The ample proposition that hope makes
In all designs begun on earth below
Fails in the promis'd largeness: checks and disasters
Grow in the veins of actions highest rear'd;
As knots, by the conflux of meeting sap,
Infect the sound pine and divert his grain
Tortive and errant from his course of growth.
Nor, princes, is it matter new to us
That we come short of our suppose so far
That after seven years' siege yet Troy walls stand;
Sith every action that hath gone before
Whereof we have record, trial did draw
Bias and thwart, not answering the aim,

And that unbodied figure of the thought
That gave't surmised shape. Why then, you princes,
Do you with cheeks abash'd behold our works,
And call them shames? which are indeed nought else
But the protractive trials of great Jove,
To find persistive constancy in men:
The fineness of which metal is not found
In Fortune's love; for then, the bold and coward,
The wise and fool, the artist and unread,
The hard and soft, seem all affin'd and kin:
But, in the wind and tempest of her frown,
Distinction, with a broad and powerful fan,
Puffing at all, winnows the light away;
And what hath mass or matter, by itself
Lies rich in virtue and unmingled.

How all occasions do inform against me,
And spur my dull revenge! What is a man,
If his chief good and market of his time
Be but to sleep and feed? a beast, no more.
Sure he that made us with such large discourse,
Looking before and after, gave us not
That capability and god-like reason
To fust in us unus'd. Now, whe'r it be
Bestial oblivion, or some craven scruple
Of thinking too precisely on the event,
A thought, which, quarter'd, hath but one part
    wisdom,

And ever three parts coward, I do not know
Why yet I live to say "This thing's to do";
Sith I have cause and will and strength and means
To do't. Examples gross as earth exhort me:
Witness this army of such mass and charge
Led by a delicate and tender prince,
Whose spirit with divine ambition puff'd
Makes mouths at the invisible event,
Exposing what is mortal and unsure
To all that fortune, death and danger dare,
Even for an egg-shell. Rightly to be great
Is not to stir without great argument,
But greatly to find quarrel in a straw
When honour's at the stake. How stand I then,
That have a father kill'd, a mother stain'd,
Excitements of my reason and my blood,
And let all sleep, while, to my shame, I see
The imminent death of twenty thousand men,
That, for a fantasy and trick of fame,
Go to their graves like beds, fight for a plot
Whereon the numbers cannot try the cause,
Which is not tomb enough and continent
To hide the slain? O! from this time forth,
My thoughts be bloody, or be nothing worth!

Time hath, my lord, a wallet at his back,
Wherein he puts alms for oblivion,
A great siz'd monster of ingratitudes:

Those scraps are good deeds past; which are
   devour'd
As fast as they are made, forgot as soon
As done: perseverance, dear my lord,
Keeps honour bright: to have done, is to hang
Quite out of fashion, like a rusty mail
In monumental mockery. Take the instant way;
For honour travels in a strait so narrow
Where one but goes abreast: keep, then, the path;
For emulation hath a thousand sons
That one by one pursue: if you give way,
Or hedge aside from the direct forthright,
Like to an enter'd tide they all rush by
And leave you hindmost;
Or, like a gallant horse fall'n in first rank,
Lie there for pavement to the abject rear,
O'errun and trampled on: then what they do in
   present,
Though less than yours in past, must o'ertop yours;
For time is like a fashionable host,
That slightly shakes his parting guest by the hand,
And with his arms outstretch'd, as he would fly,
Grasps in the comer: welcome ever smiles,
And farewell goes out sighing. O! let not virtue seek
Remuneration for the thing it was;
For beauty, wit,
High birth, vigour of bone, desert in service,
Love, friendship, charity, are subjects all
To envious and calumniating time.
One touch of nature makes the whole world kin,

That all with one consent praise new-born gawds,
Though they are made and moulded of things past,
And give to dust that is a little gilt
More laud than gilt o'er-dusted.
The present eye praises the present object.

This heavy-headed revel east and west
Makes us traduc'd and tax'd of other nations;
They clepe us drunkards, and with swinish phrase
Soil our addition; and indeed it takes
From our achievements, though perform'd at
    height,
The pith and marrow of our attribute.
So, oft it chances in particular men,
That for some vicious mole of nature in them,
As, in their birth,—wherein they are not guilty,
Since nature cannot choose his origin,—
By the o'ergrowth of some complexion,
Oft breaking down the pales and forts of reason,
Or by some habit that too much o'er-leavens
The form of plausive manners; that these men,
Carrying, I say, the stamp of one defect,
Being nature's livery, or fortune's star,
Their virtues else, be they as pure as grace,
As infinite as man may undergo,
Shall in the general censure take corruption
From that particular fault: the dram of eale

Doth all the noble substance of a doubt,
To his own scandal.

O Pandarus! I tell thee, Pandarus,—
When I do tell thee, there my hopes lie drown'd,
Reply not in how many fathoms deep
They lie indrench'd. I tell thee I am mad
In Cressid's love: thou answer'st, she is fair;
Pour'st in the open ulcer of my heart
Her eyes, her hair, her cheek, her gait, her voice;
Handlest in thy discourse, O! that her hand,
In whose comparison all whites are ink,
Writing their own reproach; to whose soft seizure
The cygnet's down is harsh, and spirit of sense
Hard as the palm of ploughman; this thou
    tell'st me,
As true thou tell'st me, when I say I love her;
But, saying thus, instead of oil and balm,
Thou lay'st in every gash that love hath given me
The knife that made it.

In the reproof of chance
Lies the true proof of men: the sea being smooth,
How many shallow bauble boats dare sail
Upon her patient breast, making their way

With those of nobler bulk!
But let the ruffian Boreas once enrage
The gentle Thetis, and anon behold
The strong-ribb'd bark through liquid mountains
    cut
Bounding between the two moist elements,
Like Perseus' horse: where's then the saucy boat
Whose weak untimber'd sides but even now
Co-rivall'd greatness? either to harbour fled,
Or made a toast for Neptune. Even so
Doth valour's show and valour's worth divide
In storms of fortune; for in her ray and brightness
The herd hath more annoyance by the breese
Than by the tiger; but when the splitting wind
Makes flexible the knees of knotted oaks,
And flies fled under shade, why then the thing of
    courage,
As rous'd with rage, with rage doth sympathize,
And with an accent tun'd in self-same key,
Retorts to chiding fortune.

To be, or not to be: that is the question:
Whether 'tis nobler in the mind to suffer
The slings and arrows of outrageous fortune,
Or to take arms against a sea of troubles,
And by opposing end them? To die: to sleep;
No more; and, by a sleep to say we end

The heart-ache and the thousand natural shocks
That flesh is heir to, 'tis a consummation
Devoutly to be wish'd. To die, to sleep;
To sleep: perchance to dream: ay, there's the rub;
For in that sleep of death what dreams may come
When we have shuffled off this mortal coil,
Must give us pause. There's the respect
That makes calamity of so long life;
For who would bear the whips and scorns of
    time,
The oppressor's wrong, the proud man's
    contumely,
The pangs of dispriz'd love, the law's delay,
The insolence of office, and the spurns
That patient merit of the unworthy takes,
When he himself might his quietus make
With a bare bodkin? who would fardels bear,
To grunt and sweat under a weary life,
But that the dread of something after death,
The undiscover'd country from whose bourn
No traveller returns, puzzles the will,
And makes us rather bear those ills we have
Than fly to others that we know not of?
Thus conscience does make cowards of us all;
And thus the native hue of resolution
Is sicklied o'er with the pale cast of thought,
And enterprises of great pith and moment
With this regard their currents turn awry,
And lose the name of action.

Could great men thunder
As Jove himself does, Jove would ne'er be quiet,
For every pelting, petty officer
Would use his heaven for thunder; nothing but
    thunder.
Merciful heaven!
Thou rather with thy sharp and sulphurous bolt
Split'st the unwedgeable and gnarled oak
Than the soft myrtle; but man, proud man,
Drest in a little brief authority,
Most ignorant of what he's most assur'd,
His glassy essence, like an angry ape,
Plays such fantastic tricks before high heaven
As make the angels weep; who, with our spleens,
Would all themselves laugh mortal.

It is the cause, it is the cause, my soul;
Let me not name it to you, you chaste stars!
It is the cause. Yet I'll not shed her blood,
Nor scar that whiter skin of hers than snow,
And smooth as monumental alabaster.
Yet she must die, else she'll betray more men.
Put out the light, and then put out the light:
If I quench thee, thou flaming minister,
I can again thy former light restore,
Should I repent me; but once put out thy light,
Thou cunning'st pattern of excelling nature,
I know not where is that Promethean heat

That can thy light relume. When I have pluck'd the
    rose,
I cannot give it vital growth again,
It needs must wither: I'll smell it on the tree.

                                        [*Kisses her.*]

O balmy breath, that dost almost persuade
Justice to break her sword! One more, one more.
Be thus when thou art dead, and I will kill thee,
And love thee after. One more, and this the last:
So sweet was ne'er so fatal.

The rugged Pyrrhus, he, whose sable arms,
Black as his purpose, did the night resemble
When he lay couched in the ominous horse,
Hath now this dread and black complexion smear'd
With heraldry more dismal; head to foot
Now is he total gules; horridly trick'd
With blood of fathers, mothers, daughters, sons,
Bak'd and impasted with the parching streets,
That lend a tyrannous and damned light
To their vile murders: roasted in wrath and fire,
And thus o'er-sized with coagulate gore,
With eyes like carbuncles, the hellish Pyrrhus
Old grandsire Priam seeks.

                                Anon, he finds him
Striking too short at Greeks; his antique sword,
Rebellious to his arm, lies where it falls,
Repugnant to command. Unequal match'd,
Pyrrhus at Priam drives; in rage strikes wide;
But with the whiff and wind of his fell sword

The unnerved father falls. Then senseless Ilium,
Seeming to feel this blow, with flaming top
Stoops to his base, and with a hideous crash
Takes prisoner Pyrrhus' ear: for lo! his sword,
Which was declining on the milky head
Of reverend Priam, seem'd i' the air to stick:
So, as a painted tyrant, Pyrrhus stood,
And like a neutral to his will and matter,
Did nothing.
But, as we often see, against some storm,
A silence in the heavens, the rack stand still,
The bold winds speechless and the orb below
As hush as death, anon the dreadful thunder
Doth rend the region; so, after Pyrrhus' pause,
Aroused vengeance set him new a-work;
And never did the Cyclops' hammers fall
On Mars's armour, forg'd for proof eterne,
With less remorse than Pyrrhus' bleeding sword
Now falls on Priam.
Out, out, thou strumpet, Fortune! All you gods,
In general synod, take away her power;
Break all the spokes and fellies from her wheel,
And bowl the round nave down the hill of heaven,
As low as to the fiends!
But who, O! who had seen the mobled queen—
Run barefoot up and down, threat'ning the flames
With bisson rheum; a clout upon that head
Where late the diadem stood; and, for a robe,
About her lank and all o'er-teemed loins,
A blanket, in the alarm of fear caught up;

Who this had seen, with tongue in venom steep'd,
'Gainst Fortune's state would treason have
    pronounc'd:
But if the gods themselves did see her then,
When she saw Pyrrhus make malicious sport
In mincing with his sword her husband's limbs,
The instant burst of clamour that she made—
Unless things mortal move them not at all—
Would have made milch the burning eyes of heaven,
And passion in the gods.

There is a willow grows aslant a brook.
That shows his hoar leaves in the glassy stream;
There with fantastic garlands did she come,
Of crow-flowers, nettles, daisies, and long purples,
That liberal shepherds give a grosser name,
But our cold maids do dead men's fingers call them:
There, on the pendent boughs her coronet weeds
Clambering to hang, an envious sliver broke,
When down her weedy trophies and herself
Fell in the weeping brook. Her clothes spread wide,
And, mermaid-like, awhile they bore her up;
Which time she chanted snatches of old tunes,
As one incapable of her own distress,
Or like a creature native and indu'd
Unto that element; but long it could not be
Till that her garments, heavy with their drink,
Pull'd the poor wretch from her melodious lay
To muddy death.

Her father lov'd me; oft invited me;
Still question'd me the story of my life
From year to year, the battles, sieges, fortunes
That I have pass'd.
I ran it through, even from my boyish days
To the very moment that he bade me tell it;
Wherein I spake of most disastrous chances,
Of moving accidents by flood and field,
Of hair-breadth 'scapes i' the imminent deadly
    breach,
Of being taken by the insolent foe
And sold to slavery, of my redemption thence
And portance in my travel's history;
Wherein of antres vast and deserts idle,
Rough quarries, rocks and hills whose heads touch
    heaven,
It was my hint to speak, such was the process;
And of the Cannibals that each other eat,
The Anthropophagi, and men whose heads
Do grow beneath their shoulders. This to hear
Would Desdemona seriously incline;
But still the house-affairs would draw her thence;
Which ever as she could with haste dispatch,
She'd come again, and with a greedy ear
Devour up my discourse. Which I observing,
Took once a pliant hour, and found good means
To draw from her a prayer of earnest heart
That I would all my pilgrimage dilate,
Whereof by parcels she had something heard,
But not intentively: I did consent;

And often did beguile her of her tears,
When I did speak of some distressful stroke
That my youth suffer'd. My story being done,
She gave me for my pains a world of sighs:
She swore, in faith, 'twas strange, 'twas passing
    strange;
'Twas pitiful, 'twas wondrous pitiful:
She wish'd she had not heard it, yet she wish'd
That heaven had made her such a man; she
    thank'd me,
And bade me, if I had a friend that lov'd her,
I should but teach him how to tell my story,
And that would woo her. Upon this hint I spake:
She lov'd me for the dangers I had pass'd,
And I lov'd her that she did pity them
This only is the witchcraft I have us'd:

O! my offence is rank, it smells to heaven;
It hath the primal eldest curse upon't;
A brother's murder! Pray can I not,
Though inclination be as sharp as will:
My stronger guilt defeats my strong intent,
And, like a man to double business bound,
I stand in pause where I shall first begin,
And both neglect. What if this cursed hand
Were thicker than itself with brother's blood,
Is there not rain enough in the sweet heavens
To wash it white as snow? Whereto serves mercy
But to confront the visage of offence?
And what's in prayer but this two-fold force,

To be forestalled, ere we come to fall,
Or pardon'd, being down? Then, I'll look up;
My fault is past. But, O! what form of prayer
Can serve my turn? "Forgive me my foul murder"?
That cannot be; since I am still possess'd
Of those effects for which I did the murder,
My crown, mine own ambition, and my queen.
May one be pardon'd and retain the offence?
In the corrupted currents of this world
Offence's gilded hand may shove by justice,
And oft 'tis seen the wicked prize itself
Buys out the law; but 'tis not so above;
There is no shuffling, there the action lies
In his true nature, and we ourselves compell'd
Even to the teeth and forehead of our faults
To give in evidence. What then? what rests?
Try what repentance can: what can it not?
Yet what can it, when one can not repent?
O wretched state! O bosom black as death!
O limed soul, that struggling to be free
Art more engaged! Help, angels! make assay;
Bow, stubborn knees; and heart with strings of
    steel
Be soft as sinews of the new-born babe.
All may be well.

—Alas! poor Yorick. I knew him, Horatio; a fellow
of infinite jest, of most excellent fancy; he hath
borne me on his back a thousand times; and now,
how abhorred in my imagination it is! my gorge

rises at it. Here hung those lips that I have kissed I know not how oft. Where be your gibes now? your gambols? your songs? your flashes of merriment, that were wont to set the table on a roar? Not one now, to mock your own grinning? quite chapfallen? Now get you to my lady's chamber, and tell her, let her paint an inch thick, to this favour she must come; make her laugh at that.

Soft you; a word or two before you go.
I have done the state some service, and they
    know't;
No more of that. I pray you, in your letters,
When you shall these unlucky deeds relate,
Speak of me as I am; nothing extenuate,
Nor set down aught in malice: then, must you
    speak
Of one that lov'd not wisely but too well;
Of one not easily jealous, but, being wrought,
Perplex'd in the extreme; of one whose hand,
Like the base Indian, threw a pearl away
Richer than all his tribe; of one whose subdu'd eyes
Albeit unused to the melting mood,
Drop tears as fast as the Arabian trees
Their med'cinable gum. Set you down this;
And say besides, that in Aleppo once,
Where a malignant and a turban'd Turk
Beat a Venetian and traduc'd the state,
I took by the throat the circumcised dog,
And smote him thus.   [*Stabs himself.*]

Thrice the brinded cat hath mew'd.

Thrice and once the hedge-pig whin'd.

Harper cries: 'Tis time, 'tis time.

Round about the cauldron go;

In the poison'd entrails throw.

Toad, that under cold stone

Days and nights hast thirty-one

Swelter'd venom sleeping got,

Boil thou first i' the charmed pot.

    Double, double toil and trouble;

      Fire burn and cauldron bubble.

Fillet of a fenny snake,

In the cauldron boil and bake;

Eye of newt, and toe of frog,

Wool of bat, and tongue of dog,

Adder's fork, and blind-worm's sting,

Lizard's leg, and howlet's wing,

For a charm of powerful trouble,

Like a hell-broth boil and bubble.

    Double, double toil and trouble;

      Fire burn and cauldron bubble.

Scale of dragon, tooth of wolf,

Witches' mummy, maw and gulf

Of the ravin'd salt-sea shark,

Root of hemlock digg'd i' the dark,

Liver of blaspheming Jew,

Gall of goat, and slips of yew

Sliver'd in the moon's eclipse,

Nose of Turk, and Tartar's lips,
Finger of birth-strangled babe
Ditch-deliver'd by a drab,
Make the gruel thick and slab:
Add thereto a tiger's chaudron,
For the ingredients of our cauldron.
    Double, double toil and trouble;
    Fire burn and cauldron bubble.
    Cool it with a baboon's blood,
    Then the charm is firm and good.

    These late eclipses in the sun and moon portend no good to us: though the wisdom of nature can reason it thus and thus, yet nature finds itself scourged by the sequent effects. Love cools, friendship falls off, brothers divide: in cities, mutinies; in countries, discord; in palaces, treason; and the bond cracked between son and father. This villain of mine comes under the prediction; there's son against father: the king falls from bias of nature; there's father against child. We have seen the best of our time: machinations, hollowness, treachery, and all ruinous disorders, follow us disquietly to our graves

The night has been unruly: where we lay,
Our chimneys were blown down; and, as they say,
Lamentings heard i' the air; strange screams of
    death,
And prophesying with accents terrible
Of dire combustion and confus'd events

New hatch'd to the woeful time. The obscure bird
Clamour'd the livelong night: some say the earth
Was feverous and did shake.

O blessed breeding sun! draw from the earth
Rotten humidity; below thy sister's orb
Infect the air! Twinn'd brothers of one womb,
Whose procreation, residence and birth,
Scarce is dividant, touch them with several fortunes;
The greater scorns the lesser: not nature,
To whom all sores lay siege, can bear great fortune,
But by contempt of nature.
Raise me this beggar, and deny't that lord;
The senator shall bear contempt hereditary,
The beggar native honour.
It is the pasture lards the rother's sides,
The want that makes him lean. Who dares, who
    dares,
In purity of manhood stand upright,
And say, "This man's a flatterer"? if one be,
So are they all; for every grize of fortune
Is smooth'd by that below: the learned pate
Ducks to the golden fool: all is oblique;
There's nothing level in our cursed natures
But direct villainy. Therefore, he abhorr'd
All feasts, societies, and throngs of men!
His semblable, yea, himself, Timon disdains:

Destruction fang mankind! Earth, yield me roots!

[*Digging.*]

Who seeks for better of thee, sauce his palate
With thy most operant poison! What is here?
Gold! yellow, glittering, precious gold! No, gods,
I am no idle votarist. Roots, you clear heavens!
Thus much of this will make black white, foul fair,
Wrong right, base noble, old young, coward valiant.
Ha! you gods, why this? What this, you gods? Why,
   this
Will lug your priests and servants from your sides,
Pluck stout men's pillows from below their head:
This yellow slave
Will knit and break religions; bless the accurs'd;
Make the hoar leprosy ador'd; place thieves,
And give them title, knee, and approbation,
With senators on the bench; this is it
That makes the wappen'd widow wed again;
She, whom the spital-house and ulcerous sores
Would cast the gorge at, this embalms and spices
To the April day again. Come, damned earth,
Thou common whore of mankind, that putt'st odds
Among the rout of nations, I will make thee
Do thy right nature.

When I do stare, see how the subject quakes.
I pardon that man's life. What was thy cause?

Adultery?
Thou shalt not die: die for adultery! No:
The wren goes to't, and the small gilded fly
Does lecher in my sight.
Let copulation thrive; for Gloucester's bastard son
Was kinder to his father than my daughters
Got 'tween the lawful sheets.
To't luxury, pell-mell! for I lack soldiers.
Behold yond simpering dame,
Whose face between her forks presageth snow;
That minces virtue, and does shake the head
To hear of pleasure's name;
The fitchew nor the soiled horse goes to't
With a more riotous appetite.
Down from the waist they are Centaurs,
Though women all above:
But to the girdle do the gods inherit,
Beneath is all the fiends':
There's hell, there's darkness, there is the
    sulphurous pit,
Burning, scalding, stench, consumption; fie, fie, fie!
    pah, pah!
Give me an ounce of civet, good apothecary, to
    sweeten my imagination.

Glamis thou art, and Cawdor; and shalt be
What thou art promis'd. Yet do I fear thy nature;

It is too full o' the milk of human kindness
To catch the nearest way; thou wouldst be great,
Art not without ambition, but without
The illness should attend it; what thou wouldst
  highly,
That thou wouldst holily; wouldst not play false,
And yet wouldst wrongly win; thou'dst have, great
  Glamis,
That which cries, "Thus thou must do, if thou
  have it";
And that which rather thou dost fear to do
Than wishest should be undone. Hie thee hither,
That I may pour my spirits in thine ear,
And chastise with the valour of my tongue
All that impedes thee from the golden round,
Which fate and metaphysical aid doth seem
To have thee crown'd withal.

If thou wert the lion, the fox would beguile thee; if thou wert the lamb, the fox would eat thee; if thou wert the fox, the lion would suspect thee, when peradventure thou wert accused by the ass; if thou wert the ass, thy dulness would torment thee, and still thou livedst but as a breakfast to the wolf; if thou wert the wolf, thy greediness would afflict thee, and oft thou shouldst hazard thy life for thy dinner; wert thou the unicorn, pride and wrath would confound thee and make thine own self the conquest of thy fury; wert thou a bear, thou wouldst be killed by the horse; wert thou a horse, thou wouldst be seized by the leopard; wert thou a leopard, thou wert german to the lion, and the spots of thy kindred were jurors on thy life; all thy safety were remotion, and thy defence absence. What beast couldst thou be, that were not subject to a beast? and what a beast art thou already, that seest not thy loss in transformation!

Thou, Nature, art my goddess; to thy law
My services are bound. Wherefore should I
Stand in the plague of custom, and permit
The curiosity of nations to deprive me,
For that I am some twelve or fourteen moonshines
Lag of a brother? Why bastard? wherefore base?
When my dimensions are as well compact,
My mind as generous, and my shape as true,
As honest madam's issue? Why brand they us
With base? with baseness? bastardy? base, base?
Who in the lusty stealth of nature take
More composition and fierce quality
Than doth, within a dull, stale, tired bed,
Go to the creating a whole tribe of fops,
Got 'tween asleep and wake? Well then,
Legitimate Edgar, I must have your land:
Our father's love is to the bastard Edmund
As to the legitimate. Fine word, "legitimate!"
Well, my legitimate, if this letter speed,
And my invention thrive, Edmund the base
Shall top the legitimate:—I grow, I prosper;
Now, gods, stand up for bastards!

—This castle hath a pleasant seat; the air
Nimbly and sweetly recommends itself
Unto our gentle senses.

                       —This guest of summer,
The temple-haunting martlet, does approve
By his lov'd mansionry that the heaven's breath
Smells wooingly here: no jutty, frieze,
Buttress, nor coign of vantage, but this bird
Hath made his pendent bed and procreant cradle:
Where they most breed and haunt, I have observ'd
The air is delicate.

—Where's the king?
—Contending with the fretful elements;
Bids the wind blow the earth into the sea,
Or swell the curled waters 'bove the main,
That things might change or cease; tears his white
    hair,
Which the impetuous blasts, with eyeless rage,
Catch in their fury, and make nothing of;
Strives in his little world of man to out-scorn
The to-and-fro-conflicting wind and rain.
This night, wherein the cub-drawn bear would couch,
The lion and the belly-pinched wolf
Keep their fur dry, unbonneted he runs,
And bids what will take all.

Was the hope drunk,
Wherein you dress'd yourself? hath it slept since,

And wakes it now, to look so green and pale
At what it did so freely? From this time
Such I account thy love. Art thou afeard
To be the same in thine own act and valour
As thou art in desire? Wouldst thou have that
Which thou esteem'st the ornament of life,
And live a coward in thine own esteem,
Letting "I dare not" wait upon "I would,"
Like the poor cat i' the adage?

                    What beast was't, then,
That made you break this enterprise to me?
When you durst do it then you were a man;
And, to be more than what you were, you would
Be so much more the man. Nor time nor place
Did then adhere, and yet you would make both:
They have made themselves, and that their
   fitness now
Does unmake you. I have given suck, and know
How tender 'tis to love the babe that milks me:
I would, while it was smiling in my face,
Have pluck'd my nipple from his boneless gums,
And dash'd the brains out, had I so sworn as you
Have done to this.

                    Let the great gods,
That keep this dreadful pother o'er our heads,
Find out their enemies now. Tremble, thou wretch,
That hast within thee undivulged crimes,

Unwhipp'd of justice; hide thee, thou bloody hand;
Thou perjur'd, and thou simular of virtue
That art incestuous; caitiff, to pieces shake,
That under covert and convenient seeming
Hast practis'd on man's life; close pent-up guilts,
Rive your concealing continents, and cry
These dreadful summoners grace. I am a man
More sinn'd against than sinning.

Speak the speech, I pray you, as I pronounced it to you, trippingly on the tongue; but if you mouth it, as many of your players do, I had as lief the town-crier spoke my lines. Nor do not saw the air too much with your hand, thus; but use all gently: for in the very torrent, tempest, and—as I may say—whirlwind of passion, you must acquire and beget a temperance, that may give it smoothness. O! it offends me to the soul to hear a robustious periwig-pated fellow tear a passion to tatters, to very rags, to split the ears of the groundlings, who for the most part are capable of nothing but inexplicable dumb-shows and noise: I would have such a fellow whipped for o'er-doing Termagant, it out-herods Herod: pray you, avoid it.

Be not too tame neither, but let your own discretion be your tutor: suit the action to the word, the word to the action; with this special observance, that you o'erstep not the modesty of nature; for anything so overdone is from the purpose of playing, whose end, both at the first and now, was and is, to hold, as 'twere, the mirror up to nature; to show virtue her own feature, scorn her own image, and the very age and body of the time his form and pressure. Now, this overdone, or come tardy off, though it make the unskilful laugh, cannot but make the judicious grieve; the censure of which one must in your allowance o'erweigh a whole theatre of others. O! there be players that I have seen play, and heard others praise, and that highly, not to speak it profanely, that, neither having the accent of Christians nor the gait of Christian, pagan, nor man, have so strutted and bellowed that I have thought some of nature's journeymen had made men and not made them well, they imitated humanity so abominably.

                                       Hold up, you sluts,
Your aprons mountant: you are not oathable,
Although, I know, you'll swear, terribly swear
Into strong shudders and to heavenly agues
The immortal gods that hear you, spare your oaths,
I'll trust to your conditions: be whores still;
And he whose pious breath seeks to convert you,
Be strong in whore, allure him, burn him up;
Let your close fire predominate his smoke,
And be no turncoats: yet may your pains, six
    months,
Be quite contrary: and thatch your poor thin roofs
With burdens of the dead; some that were hang'd,
No matter; wear them, betray with them: whore still;
Paint till a horse may mire upon your face:
A pox of wrinkles!

Consumptions sow
In hollow bones of man; strike their sharp shins,
And mar men's spurring. Crack the lawyer's voice,
That he may never more false title plead,
Nor sound his quillets shrilly: hoar the flamen,
That scolds against the quality of flesh,
And not believes himself: down with the nose,
Down with it flat; take the bridge quite away
Of him that, his particular to foresee,
Smells from the general weal: make curl'd-pate
      ruffians bald,
And let the unscarr'd braggarts of the war
Derive some pain from you: plague all,
That your activity may defeat and quell
The source of all erection. There's more gold;
Do you damn others, and let this damn you,
And ditches grave you all!

If it were done when 'tis done, then 'twere well
It were done quickly; if the assassination
Could trammel up the consequence, and catch
With his surcease success; that but this blow
Might be the be-all and the end-all here,
But here, upon this bank and shoal of time,
We'd jump the life to come. But in these cases
We still have judgment here; that we but teach
Bloody instructions, which, being taught, return
To plague the inventor; this even-handed justice

Commends the ingredients of our poison'd chalice
To our own lips. He's here in double trust:
First, as I am his kinsman and his subject,
Strong both against the deed; then, as his host,
Who should against his murderer shut the door,
Not bear the knife myself. Besides, this Duncan
Hath borne his faculties so meek, hath been
So clear in his great office, that his virtues
Will plead like angels trumpet-tongu'd against
The deep damnation of his taking-off;
And pity, like a naked new-born babe,
Striding the blast, or heaven's cherubin, hors'd
Upon the sightless couriers of the air,
Shall blow the horrid deed in every eye,
That tears shall drown the wind. I have no spur
To prick the sides of my intent, but only
Vaulting ambition, which o'er-leaps itself
And falls on the other.

Blow, winds, and crack your cheeks! rage! blow!
You cataracts and hurricanoes, spout
Till you have drench'd our steeples, drown'd the
    cocks!
You sulphurous and thought-executing fires,
Vaunt-couriers to oak-cleaving thunderbolts,
Singe my white head! And thou, all-shaking
    thunder,
Strike flat the thick rotundity o' the world!

Crack nature's moulds, all germens spill at once
That make ingrateful man!

—That which hath made them drunk hath made
    me bold,
What hath quench'd them hath given me fire. Hark!
    Peace!
It was the owl that shriek'd, the fatal bellman,
Which gives the stern'st good-night. He is about it:
The doors are open, and the surfeited grooms
Do mock their charge with snores: I have drugg'd
    their possets,
That death and nature do contend about them,
Whether they live or die.
        —Who's there? what, ho!
        —Alack! I am afraid they have awak'd,
And 'tis not done; the attempt and not the deed
Confounds us. Hark! I laid their daggers ready;
He could not miss them. Had he not resembled
My father as he slept I had done't. My husband!
        —I have done the deed. Didst thou not hear a
        noise?
        —I heard the owl scream and the crickets cry.
Did not you speak?
        —   When?
        —   Now.
        —   As I descended?
        —Ay.

—Hark! Who lies i' the second chamber?
—   Donalbain.
—[*Looking on his hands.*] This is a sorry sight.
—A foolish thought to say a sorry sight.
—There's one did laugh in's sleep, and one cried
    "Murder!"
That they did wake each other: I stood and heard
    them;
But they did say their prayers, and address'd them
Again to sleep.
    —There are two lodg'd together.
    —One cried "God bless us!" and "Amen" the
    other:
As they had seen me with these hangman's hands.
Listening their fear, I could not say "Amen,"
When they did say "God bless us!"
—   Consider it not so deeply.
    —But wherefore could not I pronounce "Amen"?
I had most need of blessing, and "Amen"
Stuck in my throat.
    —These deeds must not be thought
After these ways; so, it will make us mad.
    —Methought I heard a voice cry "Sleep no more!
Macbeth does murder sleep," the innocent sleep,
Sleep that knits up the ravell'd sleave of care,
The death of each day's life, sore labour's bath,
Balm of hurt minds, great nature's second course,
Chief nourisher in life's feast,—
—   What do you mean?
    —Still it cried, "Sleep no more!" to all the house:

"Glamis hath murder'd sleep, and therefore Cawdor
Shall sleep no more, Macbeth shall sleep no more!"

Hoy-day! what a sweep of vanity comes this way:
They dance! they are mad women.
Like madness is the glory of this life,
As this pomp shows to a little oil and root.
We make ourselves fools to disport ourselves;
And spend our flatteries to drink those men
Upon whose age we void it up again,
With poisonous spite and envy.
Who lives that's not depraved or depraves?
Who dies that bears not one spurn to their graves
Of their friend's gift?
I should fear those that dance before me now
Would one day stamp upon me: it has been done;
Men shut their doors against a setting sun.

Wisdom and goodness to the vile seem vile;
Filths savour but themselves. What have you done?
Tigers, not daughters, what have you perform'd?
A father, and a gracious aged man,
Whose reverence the head-lugg'd bear would lick,
Most barbarous, most degenerate! have you madded.
Could my good brother suffer you to do it?
A man, a prince, by him so benefited!

If that the heavens do not their visible spirits
Send quickly down to tame these vile offences,
It will come,
Humanity must perforce prey on itself,
Like monsters of the deep.

—Who gives anything to poor Tom? whom the foul fiend hath led through fire and through flame, through ford and whirlpool, o'er bog and quagmire; that hath laid knives under his pillow, and halters in his pew; set ratsbane by his porridge; made him proud of heart, to ride on a bay trotting-horse over four-inched bridges, to course his own shadow for a traitor. Bless thy five wits! Tom's a-cold: O! do de, do de, do de. Bless thee from whirlwinds, star-blasting, and taking! Do poor Tom some charity, whom the foul fiend vexes. There could I have him now, and there, and there again, and there.

Take heed o' the foul fiend. Obey thy parents; keep thy word justly; swear not; commit not with man's sworn spouse; set not thy sweet heart on proud array. Tom's a-cold.

—What hast thou been?

—A servingman, proud in heart and mind; that curled my hair, wore gloves in my cap, served the lust of my mistress's heart, and did the act of darkness with her; swore as many oaths as I spake words, and broke them in the sweet face of heaven; one that slept in the contriving of lust, and waked to do it. Wine loved

I deeply, dice dearly, and in woman out-paramoured the Turk: false of heart, light of ear, bloody of hand; hog in sloth, fox in stealth, wolf in greediness, dog in madness, lion in prey. Let not the creaking of shoes nor the rustling of silks betray thy poor heart to woman: keep thy foot out of brothels, thy hand out of plackets, thy pen from lenders' books, and defy the foul fiend. Still through the hawthorn blows the cold wind; says suum, mun ha no nonny. Dolphin my boy, my boy, sessa! let him trot by.

—What are you there? Your names?

—Poor Tom; that eats the swimming frog; the toad, the tadpole, the wall-newt, and the water; that in the fury of his heart, when the foul fiend rages, eats cow-dung for sallets; swallows the old rat and the ditch-dog; drinks the green mantle of the standing pool; who is whipped from tithing to tithing, and stock punished, and imprisoned; who hath had three suits to his back, six shirts to his body, horse to ride, and weapon to wear;

> But mice and rats and such small deer
> Have been Tom's food for seven long year.

Beware my follower. Peace, Smulkin! peace, thou fiend.

We have scotch'd the snake, not kill'd it:
She'll close and be herself, whilst our poor malice

Remains in danger of her former tooth.
But let the frame of things disjoint, both the worlds
    suffer,
Ere we will eat our meal in fear, and sleep
In the affliction of these terrible dreams
That shake us nightly. Better be with the dead,
Whom we, to gain our peace, have sent to peace,
Than on the torture of the mind to lie
In restless ecstasy. Duncan is in his grave;
After life's fitful fever he sleeps well;
Treason has done his worst: nor steel, nor poison,
Malice domestic, foreign levy, nothing
Can touch him further.

Let me look back upon thee. O thou wall,
That girdlest in those wolves, dive in the earth,
And fence not Athens! Matrons, turn incontinent!
Obedience fail in children! slaves and fools,
Pluck the grave wrinkled senate from the bench,
And minister in their steads! To general filths
Convert, o' the instant, green virginity!
Do't in your parents' eyes! Bankrupts, hold fast;
Rather than render back, out with your knives,
And cut your trusters' throats! Bound servants,
    steal!—
Large-handed robbers your grave masters are,—
And pill by law. Maid, to thy master's bed;
Thy mistress is o' the brothel! Son of sixteen,

Pluck the lin'd crutch from thy old limping sire,
With it beat out his brains! Piety, and fear,
Religion to the gods, peace, justice, truth,
Domestic awe, night-rest and neighbourhood,
Instruction, manners, mysteries and trades,
Degrees, observances, customs and laws,
Decline to your confounding contraries,
And let confusion live! Plagues incident to men,
Your potent and infectious fevers heap
On Athens, ripe for stroke! Thou cold sciatica,
Cripple our senators, that their limbs may halt
As lamely as their manners! Lust and liberty
Creep in the minds and marrows of our youth,
That 'gainst the stream of virtue they may strive,
And drown themselves in riot! Itches, blains,
Sow all the Athenian bosoms, and their crop
Be general leprosy! Breath infect breath,
That their society, as their friendship, may
Be merely poison! Nothing I'll bear from thee
But nakedness, thou detestable town!
Take thou that too, with multiplying bans!
Timon will to the woods; where he shall find
The unkindest beast more kinder than mankind.

This is the excellent foppery of the world, that, when we are sick in fortune,—often the surfeit of our own behaviour,—we make guilty of our disasters the sun, the moon, and the stars; as if we were villains by necessity, fools by heavenly compulsion, knaves, thieves, and treachers by spherical predominance, drunkards, liars, and adulterers by an enforced obedience of planetary influence; and all that we are evil in, by a divine thrusting on: an admirable evasion of whoremaster man, to lay his goatish disposition to the charge of a star! My father compounded with my mother under the dragon's tail, and my nativity was under *ursa major;* so that it follows I am rough and lecherous. 'Sfoot! I should have been that I am had the maidenliest star in the firmament twinkled on my bastardizing.

A man may see how this world goes with no eyes. Look with thine ears: see how yond justice rails upon yon simple thief. Hark, in thine ear: change places; and, handy-dandy, which is the justice, which is the thief? Thou hast seen a farmer's dog bark at a beggar?

And the creature run from the cur? There thou mightst behold the great image of authority; a dog's obey'd in office.

Thou rascal beadle, hold thy bloody hand!

Why dost thou lash that whore? Strip thine own back;

Thou hotly lust'st to use her in that kind

For which thou whipp'st her. The usurer hangs the cozener.

Through tatter'd clothes small vices do appear;

Robes and furr'd gowns hide all. Plate sin with gold,

And the strong lance of justice hurtless breaks;

Arm it in rags, a pigmy's straw doth pierce it.
None does offend, none, I say none; I'll able 'em:
Take that of me, my friend, who have the power
To seal the accuser's lips. Get thee glass eyes;
And, like a scurvy politician, seem
To see the things thou dost not.

Poor naked wretches, wheresoe'er you are,
That bide the pelting of this pitiless storm,
How shall your houseless heads and unfed sides,
Your loop'd and window'd raggedness, defend you
From seasons such as these? O! I have ta'en
Too little care of this. Take physic, pomp;
Expose thyself to feel what wretches feel,
That thou mayst shake the superflux to them,
And show the heavens more just.

Put up thy gold: go on, — here's gold, — go on;
Be as a planetary plague, when Jove
Will o'er some high-vic'd city hang his poison
In the sick air: let not thy sword skip one.
Pity not honour'd age for his white beard;
He is a usurer. Strike me the counterfeit matron;
It is her habit only that is honest,
Herself's a bawd. Let not the virgin's cheek
Make soft thy trenchant sword; for those milk-paps,

That through the window-bars bore at men's eyes,
Are not within the leaf of pity writ,
But set them down horrible traitors. Spare not the
   babe,
Whose dimpled smiles from fools exhaust their
   mercy;
Think it a bastard, whom the oracle
Hath doubtfully pronounc'd thy throat shall cut,
And mince it sans remorse. Swear against objects;
Put armour on thine ears and on thine eyes,
Whose proof nor yells of mothers, maids, nor babes,
Nor sight of priests in holy vestments bleeding,
Shall pierce a jot. There's gold to pay thy soldiers:
Make large confusion; and, thy fury spent,
Confounded be thyself!

Had I but died an hour before this chance
I had liv'd a blessed time; for, from this instant,
There's nothing serious in mortality,
All is but toys; renown and grace is dead,
The wine of life is drawn, and the mere lees
Is left this vault to brag of.

O! reason not the need; our basest beggars
Are in the poorest thing superfluous:
Allow not nature more than nature needs,

Man's life is cheap as beast's. Thou art a lady;
If only to go warm were gorgeous,
Why, nature needs not what thou gorgeous wear'st,
Which scarcely keeps thee warm. But, for true
    need,—
You heavens, give me that patience, patience I need!
You see me here, you gods, a poor old man,
As full of grief as age; wretched in both!
If it be you that stir these daughters' hearts
Against their father, fool me not so much
To bear it tamely; touch me with noble anger,
And let not women's weapons, water-drops,
Stain my man's cheeks! No, you unnatural hags,
I will have such revenges on you both
That all the world shall—I will do such things,—
What they are yet I know not,—but they shall be
The terrors of the earth. You think I'll weep;
No, I'll not weep:
I have full cause of weeping, but this heart
Shall break into a hundred thousand flaws
Or ere I'll weep. O fool! I shall go mad.

The raven himself is hoarse
That croaks the fatal entrance of Duncan
Under my battlements. Come, you spirits
That tend on mortal thoughts! unsex me here,
And fill me from the crown to the toe top full
Of direst cruelty; make thick my blood,

Stop up the access and passage to remorse,
That no compunctious visitings of nature
Shake my fell purpose, nor keep peace between
The effect and it! Come to my woman's breasts,
And take my milk for gall, you murdering
    ministers,
Wherever in your sightless substances
You wait on nature's mischief! Come, thick night,
And pall thee in the dunnest smoke of hell,
That my keen knife see not the wound it makes,
Nor heaven peep through the blanket of the dark,
To cry, "Hold, hold!"

—What three things does drink especially provoke?

—Marry, sir, nose-painting, sleep, and urine. Lechery, sir, it provokes, and unprovokes; it provokes the desire, but it takes away the performance. Therefore much drink may be said to be an equivocator with lechery; it makes him, and it mars him; it sets him on, and it takes him off; it persuades him, and disheartens him; makes him stand to, and not stand to; in conclusion, equivocates him in a sleep, and, giving him the lie, leaves him.

Hear, Nature, hear! dear goddess, hear!
Suspend thy purpose, if thou didst intend
To make this creature fruitful!
Into her womb convey sterility!
Dry up in her the organs of increase,

And from her derogate body never spring
A babe to honour her! If she must teem,
Create her child of spleen, that it may live
And be a thwart disnatur'd torment to her!
Let it stamp wrinkles in her brow of youth,
With cadent tears fret channels in her cheeks,
Turn all her mother's pains and benefits
To laughter and contempt, that she may feel
How sharper than a serpent's tooth it is
To have a thankless child!
Common mother, thou,   [*Digging.*]
Whose womb unmeasurable, and infinite breast,
Teems, and feeds all; whose self-same mettle,
Whereof thy proud child, arrogant man, is puff'd,
Engenders the black toad and adder blue,
The gilded newt and eyeless venom'd worm,
With all the abhorred births below crisp heaven
Whereon Hyperion's quickening fire doth shine;
Yield him, who all thy human sons doth hate,
From forth thy plenteous bosom, one poor root!
Ensear thy fertile and conceptious womb,
Let it no more bring out ingrateful man!
Go great with tigers, dragons, wolves, and bears;
Teem with new monsters, whom thy upward face
Hath to the marbled mansion all above
Never presented! O! a root; dear thanks:
Dry up thy marrows, vines and plough-torn leas;
Whereof ingrateful man, with liquorish draughts
And morsels unctuous, greases his pure mind,
That from it all consideration slips!

Why, thou wert better in thy grave than to answer
with thy uncovered body this extremity of the skies.
Is man no more than this? Consider him well.
Thou owest the worm no silk, the beast no hide,
the sheep no wool, the cat no perfume. Ha! here's
three on's are sophisticated; thou art the thing itself;
unaccommodated man is no more but such a poor,
bare, forked animal as thou art. Off, off, you lendings!
Come, unbutton here.

Thou hast cast away thyself, being like thyself;
A madman so long, now a fool. What! think'st
That the bleak air, thy boisterous chamberlain,
Will put thy shirt on warm? will these moss'd trees,
That have outliv'd the eagle, page thy heels
And skip when thou point'st out? will the cold
   brook,
Candied with ice, caudle thy morning taste
To cure the o'er-night's surfeit? Call the creatures
Whose naked natures live in all the spite
Of wreakful heaven, whose bare unhoused trunks
To the conflicting elements expos'd,
Answer mere nature; bid them flatter thee.

                        How fearful
And dizzy 'tis to cast one's eyes so low!
The crows and choughs that wing the midway air

Show scarce so gross as beetles; half way down
Hangs one that gathers samphire, dreadful trade!
Methinks he seems no bigger than his head.
The fishermen that walk upon the beach
Appear like mice, and yond tall anchoring bark
Diminish'd to her cock, her cock a buoy
Almost too small for sight. The murmuring surge,
That on the unnumber'd idle pebbles chafes,
Cannot be heard so high. I'll look no more,
Lest my brain turn, and the deficient sight
Topple down headlong.

Is this a dagger which I see before me,
The handle toward my hand? Come, let me clutch
    thee:
I have thee not, and yet I see thee still.
Art thou not, fatal vision, sensible
To feeling as to sight? or art thou but
A dagger of the mind, a false creation,
Proceeding from the heat-oppressed brain?
I see thee yet, in form as palpable
As this which now I draw.
Thou marshall'st me the way that I was going;
And such an instrument I was to use.
Mine eyes are made the fools o' the other senses,
Or else worth all the rest: I see thee still;
And on thy blade and dudgeon gouts of blood,

Which was not so before. There's no such thing:
It is the bloody business which informs
Thus to mine eyes. Now o'er the one half-world
Nature seems dead, and wicked dreams abuse
The curtain'd sleep; witchcraft celebrates
Pale Hecate's offerings; and wither'd murder,
Alarum'd by his sentinel, the wolf,
Whose howl's his watch, thus with his stealthy
     pace,
With Tarquin's ravishing strides, toward his design
Moves like a ghost. Thou sure and firm-set earth,
Hear not my steps, which way they walk, for fear
The very stones prate of my whereabout,
And take the present horror from the time,
Which now suits with it.

No, no, no, no! Come, let's away to prison;
We two alone will sing like birds i' the cage:
When thou dost ask me blessing, I'll kneel down,
And ask of thee forgiveness: so we'll live,
And pray, and sing, and tell old tales, and laugh
At gilded butterflies, and hear poor rogues
Talk of court news; and we'll talk with them too,
Who loses and who wins; who's in, who's out;
And take upon's the mystery of things,
As if we were God's spies: and we'll wear out,
In a wall'd prison, packs and sects of great ones
That ebb and flow by the moon.

—The queen, my lord, is dead.
—She should have died hereafter;
There would have been a time for such a word.
To-morrow, and to-morrow, and to-morrow,
Creeps in this petty pace from day to day,
To the last syllable of recorded time;
And all our yesterdays have lighted fools
The way to dusty death. Out, out, brief candle!
Life's but a walking shadow, a poor player
That struts and frets his hour upon the stage,
And then is heard no more; it is a tale
Told by an idiot, full of sound and fury,
Signifying nothing.

I have liv'd long enough: my way of life
Is fall'n into the sear, the yellow leaf;
And that which should accompany old age,
As honour, love, obedience, troops of friends,
I must not look to have; but, in their stead,
Curses, not loud but deep, mouth-honour, breath,
Which the poor heart would fain deny, and
    dare not.

Thou God of this great vast, rebuke these surges,
Which wash both heaven and hell; and thou, that
    hast

Upon the winds command, bind them in brass,
Having call'd them from the deep. O! still
Thy deafening, dreadful thunders; gently quench
Thy nimble, sulphurous flashes. O! how Lychorida,
How does my queen? Thou stormest venomously;
Wilt thou spit all thyself? The seaman's whistle
Is as a whisper in the ears of death,
Unheard. Lychorida! Lucina, O!
Divinest patroness, and midwife gentle
To those that cry by night, convey thy deity
Aboard our dancing boat; make swift the pangs
Of my queen's travails!

Be not afeard: the isle is full of noises,
Sounds and sweet airs, that give delight, and
    hurt not.
Sometimes a thousand twangling instruments
Will hum about mine ears; and sometime voices,
That, if I then had wak'd after long sleep,
Will make me sleep again: and then, in dreaming,
The clouds methought would open and show riches
Ready to drop upon me; that, when I wak'd
I cried to dream again.

The barge she sat in, like a burnish'd throne,
Burn'd on the water; the poop was beaten gold,

Purple the sails, and so perfumed, that
The winds were love-sick with them, the oars were
    silver,
Which to the tune of flutes kept stroke, and made
The water which they beat to follow faster,
As amorous of their strokes. For her own person,
It beggar'd all description; she did lie
In her pavilion,—cloth-of-gold of tissue,—
O'er-picturing that Venus where we see
The fancy outwork nature; on each side her
Stood pretty-dimpled boys, like smiling Cupids,
With divers-colour'd fans, whose wind did seem
To glow the delicate cheeks which they did cool,
And what they undid did.
Her gentlewomen, like the Nereides,
So many mermaids, tended her i' the eyes,
And made their bends adornings; at the helm
A seeming mermaid steers; the silken tackle
Swell with the touches of those flower-soft hands,
That yarely frame the office. From the barge
A strange invisible perfume hits the sense
Of the adjacent wharfs. The city cast
Her people out upon her, and Antony,
Enthron'd i' the market-place, did sit alone,
Whistling to the air; which, but for vacancy,
Had gone to gaze on Cleopatra too
And made a gap in nature.
Upon her landing, Antony sent to her,
Invited her to supper; she replied
It should be better he became her guest,

Which she entreated. Our courteous Antony,
Whom ne'er the word of "No" woman heard speak,
Being barber'd ten times o'er, goes to the feast,
And, for his ordinary pays his heart
For what his eyes eat only.

                          I saw her once
Hop forty paces through the public street;
And having lost her breath, she spoke, and panted
That she did make defect perfection,
And, breathless, power breathe forth.
Age cannot wither her, nor custom stale
Her infinite variety; other women cloy
The appetites they feed, but she makes hungry
Where most she satisfies; for vilest things
Become themselves in her, that the holy priests
Bless her when she is riggish.

What! are men mad? Hath nature given them eyes
To see this vaulted arch, and the rich crop
Of sea and land, which can distinguish 'twixt
The fiery orbs above and the twinn'd stones
Upon the number'd beach? and can we not
Partition make with spectacles so precious
'Twixt fair and foul?
It cannot be i' the eye; for apes and monkeys
'Twixt two such shes would chatter this way and
Contemn with mows the other; nor i' the judgment,
For idiots in this case of favour would

Be wisely definite; nor i' the appetite;
Sluttery to such neat excellence oppos'd
Should make desire vomit emptiness,
Not so allur'd to feed.

                                    The cloyed will, —
That satiate yet unsatisfied desire, that tub
Both fill'd and running, — ravening first the lamb,
Longs after for the garbage.

What you do
Still betters what is done. When you speak, sweet,
I'd have you do it ever: when you sing,
I'd have you buy and sell so; so give alms;
Pray so; for the ordering your affairs,
To sing them too: when you do dance, I wish you
A wave o' the sea, that you might ever do
Nothing but that; move still, still so,
And own no other function: each your doing,
So singular in each particular,
Crowns what you are doing in the present deed,
That all your acts are queens.

This double worship,
Where one part does disdain with cause, the other
Insult without all reason; where gentry, title,
    wisdom,

Cannot conclude, but by the yea and no
Of general ignorance,—it must omit
Real necessities, and give way the while
To unstable slightness: purpose so barr'd, it follows
Nothing is done to purpose. Therefore, beseech
    you,—
You that will be less fearful than discreet,
That love the fundamental part of state
More than you doubt the change on't, that prefer
A noble life before a long, and wish
To jump a body with a dangerous physic
That's sure of death without it, at once pluck out
The multitudinous tongue; let them not lick
The sweet which is their poison. Your dishonour
Mangles true judgment, and bereaves the state
Of that integrity which should become it,
Not having the power to do the good it would,
For the ill which doth control't.

                              Dost thou forget
From what a torment I did free thee?
Thou dost; and think'st it much to tread the ooze
Of the salt deep,
To run upon the sharp wind of the north,
To do me business in the veins o' th' earth
When it is bak'd with frost.
Hast thou forgot

The foul witch Sycorax, who with age and envy
Was grown into a hoop? hast thou forgot her?

                                    I must,
Once in a month, recount what thou hast been,
Which thou forget'st. This damn'd witch, Sycorax,
For mischiefs manifold and sorceries terrible
To enter human hearing, from Argier,
Thou know'st, was banish'd: for one thing she did
They would not take her life. Is not this true?
This blue-ey'd hag was hither brought with child
And here was left by the sailors. Thou, my slave,
As thou report'st thyself, wast then her servant:
And, for thou wast a spirit too delicate
To act her earthy and abhorr'd commands,
Refusing her grand hests, she did confine thee,
By help of her more potent ministers,
And in her most unmitigable rage,
Into a cloven pine; within which rift
Imprison'd, thou didst painfully remain
A dozen years; within which space she died
And left thee there, where thou didst vent thy
    groans
As fast as mill-wheels strike. Then was this island,—
Save for the son that she did litter here,
A freckled whelp hag-born,—not honour'd with
A human shape.

                        He that Caliban,
Whom now I keep in service. Thou best know'st
What torment I did find thee in; thy groans

Did make wolves howl and penetrate the breasts
Of ever-angry bears: it was a torment
To lay upon the damn'd, which Sycorax
Could not again undo; it was mine art,
When I arriv'd and heard thee, that made gape
The pine, and let thee out.
If thou more murmur'st, I will rend an oak
And peg thee in his knotty entrails till
Thou hast howl'd away twelve winters.

Where think'st thou he is now? Stands he, or
        sits he?
Or does he walk? or is he on his horse?
O happy horse, to bear the weight of Antony!
Do bravely, horse, for wot'st thou whom thou
        mov'st?
The demi-Atlas of this earth, the arm
And burgonet of men. He's speaking now,
Or murmuring "Where's my serpent of old Nile?"
For so he calls me. Now I feed myself
With most delicious poison. Think on me,
That am with Phœbus' amorous pinches black,
And wrinkled deep in time? Broad-fronted Cæsar,
When thou wast here above the ground I was
A morsel for a monarch, and great Pompey
Would stand and make his eyes grow in my brow;
There would he anchor his aspect and die
With looking on his life.

You common cry of curs! whose breath I hate
As reek o' the rotten fens, whose loves I prize
As the dead carcases of unburied men
That do corrupt my air, I banish you;
And here remain with your uncertainty!
Let every feeble rumour shake your hearts!
Your enemies, with nodding of their plumes,
Fan you into despair! Have the power still
To banish your defenders; till at length
Your ignorance, — which finds not, till it feels, —
Making but reservation of yourselves, —
Still your own foes, — deliver you as most
Abated captives to some nation
That won you without blows! Despising,
For you, the city, thus I turn my back:
There is a world elsewhere.

He no more remembers his mother now than
an eight-year-old horse. The tartness of his face
sours ripe grapes: when he walks, he moves like an
engine, and the ground shrinks before his treading:
he is able to pierce a corslet with his eye; talks like a
knell, and his hum is a battery. He sits in his state, as
a thing made for Alexander. What he bids be done is
finished with his bidding. He wants nothing of a god
but eternity and a heaven to throne in.

Had I this cheek
To bathe my lips upon; this hand, whose touch,
Whose every touch, would force the feeler's soul

To the oath of loyalty; this object, which
Takes prisoner the wild motion of mine eye,
Fixing it only here; should I—damn'd then—
Slaver with lips as common as the stairs
That mount the Capitol; join gripes with hands
Made hard with hourly falsehood,—falsehood, as
With labour;—then by-peeping in an eye,
Base and illustrous as the smoky light
That's fed with stinking tallow; it were fit
That all the plagues of hell should at one time
Encounter such revolt.

He that will give good words to thee will flatter
Beneath abhorring. What would you have, you curs,
That like nor peace nor war? the one affrights you,
The other makes you proud. He that trusts to you,
Where he should find you lions, finds you hares;
Where foxes, geese: you are no surer, no,
Than is the coal of fire upon the ice,
Or hailstone in the sun. Your virtue is,
To make him worthy whose offence subdues him,
And curse that justice did it. Who deserves greatness
Deserves your hate; and your affections are
A sick man's appetite, who desires most that
Which would increase his evil. He that depends
Upon your favours swims with fins of lead
And hews down oaks with rushes. Hang ye! Trust ye?
With every minute you do change a mind,

And call him noble that was now your hate,
Him vile that was your garland.

                    O, it is monstrous! monstrous!
Methought the billows spoke and told me of it;
The winds did sing it to me; and the thunder,
That deep and dreadful organ-pipe, pronounc'd
The name of Prosper: it did bass my trespass.
Therefore my son i' th' ooze is bedded; and
I'll seek him deeper than e'er plummet sounded.
And with him there lie mudded.

All places yield to him ere he sits down;
And the nobility of Rome are his:
The senators and patricians love him too:
The tribunes are no soldiers; and their people
Will be as rash in the repeal as hasty
To expel him thence. I think he'll be to Rome
As is the osprey to the fish, who takes it
By sovereignty of nature. First he was
A noble servant to them, but he could not
Carry his honours even; whether 'twas pride,
Which out of daily fortune ever taints
The happy man; whether defect of judgment,
To fail in the disposing of those chances
Which he was lord of; or whether nature,

Not to be other than one thing, not moving
From the casque to the cushion, but commanding
    peace
Even with the same austerity and garb
As he controll'd the war; but one of these,
As he hath spices of them all, not all,
For I dare so far free him, made him fear'd,
So hated, and so banish'd: but he has a merit
To choke it in the utterance. So our virtues
Lie in the interpretation of the time;
And power, unto itself most commendable,
Hath not a tomb so evident as a chair
To extol what it hath done.

                        Is whispering nothing?
Is leaning cheek to cheek? is meeting noses?
Kissing with inside lip? stopping the career
Of laughter with a sigh?—a note infallible
Of breaking honesty,—horsing foot on foot?
Skulking in corners? wishing clocks more swift?
Hours, minutes? noon, midnight? and all eyes
Blind with the pin and web but theirs, theirs only,
That would unseen be wicked? is this nothing?
Why, then the world and all that's in't is nothing;
The covering sky is nothing; Bohemia nothing;
My wife is nothing; nor nothing have these
    nothings,
If this be nothing.

I would I had some flowers o' the spring that might
Become your time of day; and yours, and yours,
That wear upon your virgin branches yet
Your maidenheads growing: O Proserpina!
For the flowers now that frighted thou let'st fall
From Dis's waggon! daffodils,
That come before the swallow dares, and take
The winds of March with beauty; violets dim,
But sweeter than the lids of Juno's eyes
Or Cytherea's breath; pale prime-roses,
That die unmarried, ere they can behold
Bright Phœbus in his strength, a malady
Most incident to maids; bold oxlips and
The crown imperial; lilies of all kinds,
The flower-de-luce being one. O! these I lack
To make you garlands of, and my sweet friend,
To strew him o'er and o'er!

Antony,
Leave thy lascivious wassails. When thou once
Wast beaten from Modena, where thou slew'st
Hirtius and Pansa, consuls, at thy heel
Did famine follow, whom thou fought'st against,
Though daintily brought up, with patience more
Than savages could suffer; thou didst drink
The stale of horses and the gilded puddle
Which beasts would cough at; thy palate then did
    deign

The roughest berry on the rudest hedge;
Yea, like the stag, when snow the pasture sheets,
The barks of trees thou browsed'st; on the Alps
It is reported thou didst eat strange flesh,
Which some did die to look on; and all this—
It wounds thy honour that I speak it now—
Was borne so like a soldier, that thy cheek
So much as lank'd not.

Inch-thick, knee-deep, o'er head and ears a
    fork'd one!
Go play, boy, play; thy mother plays, and I
Play too, but so disgrac'd a part, whose issue
Will hiss me to my grave: contempt and clamour
Will be my knell. Go play, boy, play. There have
    been,
Or I am much deceiv'd, cuckolds ere now;
And many a man there is even at this present,
Now, while I speak this, holds his wife by the arm,
That little thinks she has been sluic'd in's absence,
And his pond fish'd by his next neighbour, by
Sir Smile, his neighbour: nay, there's comfort in't,
Whiles other men have gates, and those gates
    open'd,
As mine, against their will. Should all despair
That have revolted wives the tenth of mankind
Would hang themselves. Physic for't there is none;
It is a bawdy planet, that will strike

Where 'tis predominant; and 'tis powerful, think it,
From east, west, north, and south: be it concluded,
No barricado for a belly: know't;
It will let in and out the enemy
With bag and baggage. Many a thousand on's
Have the disease and feel't not.

When daffodils begin to peer,
    With heigh! the doxy, over the dale,
Why, then comes in the sweet o' the year;
    For the red blood reigns in the winter's pale.

The white sheet bleaching on the hedge,
    With heigh! the sweet birds, O, how they sing!
Doth set my pugging tooth on edge;
    For a quart of ale is a dish for a king.

The lark, that tirra-lirra chants,
    With, heigh! with, heigh! the thrush and the jay,
Are summer songs for me and my aunts,
    While we lie tumbling in the hay.

The crickets sing, and man's o'er-labour'd sense
Repairs itself by rest. Our Tarquin thus
Did softly press the rushes ere he waken'd
The chastity he wounded. Cytherea,

How bravely thou becom'st thy bed! fresh lily,
And whiter than the sheets! That I might touch!
But kiss: one kiss! Rubies unparagon'd,
How dearly they do't! 'Tis her breathing that
Perfumes the chamber thus; the flame of the taper
Bows toward her, and would under-peep her lids,
To see the enclosed lights, now canopied
Under these windows, white and azure lac'd
With blue of heaven's own tinct. But my design,
To note the chamber: I will write all down:
Such and such pictures; there the window; such
Th' adornment of her bed; the arras, figures,
Why, such and such; and the contents o' the story.
Ah! but some natural notes about her body,
Above ten thousand meaner moveables
Would testify, to enrich mine inventory.
O sleep! thou ape of death, lie dull upon her;
And be her senses but as a monument
Thus in a chapel lying. Come off, come off;—

       [*Taking off her bracelet.*]

As slippery as the Gordian knot was hard!
'Tis mine; and this will witness outwardly,
As strongly as the conscience does within,
To the madding of her lord. On her left breast
A mole cinque-spotted, like the crimson drops
I' the bottom of a cowslip: here's a voucher;
Stronger than ever law could make: this secret
Will force him think I have pick'd the lock and ta'en
The treasure of her honour. No more. To what end?
Why should I write this down, that's riveted,

Screw'd to my memory? She hath been reading late
The tale of Tereus; here the leaf's turn'd down
Where Philomel gave up. I have enough:
To the trunk again, and shut the spring of it.
Swift, swift, you dragons of the night, that dawning
May bare the raven's eye! I lodge in fear;
Though this a heavenly angel, hell is here.

[*Clock strikes.*]

One, two, three: time, time!

I saw him beat the surges under him,
And ride upon their backs: he trod the water,
Whose enmity he flung aside, and breasted
The surge most swoln that met him: his bold head
'Bove the contentious waves he kept, and oar'd
Himself with his good arms in lusty stroke
To the shore, that o'er his wave-worn basis bow'd,
As stooping to relieve him. I not doubt
He came alive to land.

Is there no way for men to be, but women
Must be half-workers? We are all bastards; all,
And that most venerable man which I
Did call my father was I know not where
When I was stamp'd; some coiner with his tools
Made me a counterfeit; yet my mother seem'd

The Dian of that time; so doth my wife
The nonpareil of this. O! vengeance, vengeance;
Me of my lawful pleasure she restrain'd
And pray'd me oft forbearance; did it with
A pudency so rosy the sweet view on't
Might well have warm'd old Saturn; that I
   thought her
As chaste as unsunn'd snow. O! all the devils!
This yellow Iachimo, in an hour,—was't not?
Or less—at first?—perchance he spoke not, but
Like a full-acorn'd boar, a German one,
Cried "O!" and mounted; found no opposition
But what he look'd for should oppose and she
Should from encounter guard. Could I find out
The woman's part in me! For there's no motion
That tends to vice in man but I affirm
It is the woman's part; be it lying, note it,
The woman's; flattering, hers; deceiving, hers;
Lust and rank thoughts, hers, hers; revenges, hers;
Ambitions, covetings, change of prides, disdain,
Nice longing, slanders, mutability,
All faults that man may name, nay, that hell knows,
Why, hers, in part, or all; but rather, all;
For even to vice
They are not constant, but are changing still
One vice but of a minute old for one
Not half so old as that. I'll write against them,
Detest them, curse them. Yet 'tis greater skill
In a true hate to pray they have their will:
The very devils cannot plague them better.

If by your art, my dearest father, you have
Put the wild waters in this roar, allay them.
The sky, it seems, would pour down stinking pitch,
But that the sea, mounting to th' welkin's cheek,
Dashes the fire out. O! I have suffer'd
With those that I saw suffer: a brave vessel,
Who had, no doubt, some noble creatures in her,
Dash'd all to pieces. O! the cry did knock
Against my very heart. Poor souls, they perish'd.
Had I been any god of power, I would
Have sunk the sea within the earth, or e'er
It should the good ship so have swallow'd and
The fraughting souls within her.

                                        These three,
Three thousand confident, in act as many,—
For three performers are the file when all
The rest do nothing,—with this word, "Stand,
    stand!"
Accommodated by the place, more charming
With their own nobleness,—which could have
    turn'd
A distaff to a lance,—gilded pale looks,
Part shame, part spirit renew'd; that some, turn'd
    coward
But by example,—O! a sin of war,
Damn'd in the first beginners,—'gan to look
The way that they did, and to grin like lions

Upon the pikes o' the hunters. Then began
A stop i' the chaser, a retire, anon,
A rout, confusion thick; forthwith they fly
Chickens, the way which they stoop'd eagles;
    slaves,
The strides they victors made. And now our
    cowards—
Like fragments in hard voyages—became
The life o' the need; having found the back door
    open
Of the unguarded hearts, Heavens! how they
    wound;
Some slain before; some dying; some their friends
O'er-borne i' the former wave; ten, chas'd by one,
Are now each one the slaughter-man of twenty;
Those that would die or ere resist are grown
The mortal bugs o' the field.

There was a time when all the body's members
Rebell'd against the belly; thus accus'd it:
That only like a gulf it did remain
I' the midst o' the body, idle and unactive,
Still cupboarding the viand, never bearing
Like labour with the rest, where the other
    instruments
Did see and hear, devise, instruct, walk, feel,
And, mutually participate, did minister

Unto the appetite and affection common
Of the whole body. The belly answer'd,—

                  With a kind of smile,
Which ne'er came from the lungs, but even thus—
For, look you, I may make the belly smile
As well as speak—it tauntingly replied
To the discontented members, the mutinous parts
That envied his receipt; even so most fitly
As you malign our senators for that
They are not such as you.
Note me this, good friend;
Your most grave belly was deliberate,
Not rash like his accusers, and thus answer'd:
"True is it, my incorporate friends," quoth he,
"That I receive the general food at first,
Which you do live upon; and fit it is;
Because I am the store-house and the shop
Of the whole body: but, if you do remember,
I send it through the rivers of your blood,
Even to the court, the heart, to the seat o' the brain;
And, through the cranks and offices of man,
The strongest nerves and small inferior veins
From me receive that natural competency
Whereby they live. And though that all at once,
You, my good friends,"—this says the belly, mark
    me.—

                "Though all at once cannot
See what I do deliver out to each,
Yet I can make my audit up, that all

From me do back receive the flour of all,
And leave me but the bran."

Fear no more the heat o' the sun,
    Nor the furious winter's rages;
Thou thy worldly task hast done,
    Home art gone, and ta'en thy wages;
Golden lads and girls all must
    As chimney-sweepers, come to dust.

Fear no more the frown o' the great,
    Thou art past the tyrant's stroke:
Care no more to clothe and eat;
    To thee the reed is as the oak;
The sceptre, learning, physic, must
    All follow this, and come to dust.

Fear no more the lightning-flash,
    Nor the all-dreaded thunder-stone;
Fear not slander, censure rash;
    Thou hast finish'd joy and moan:
All lovers young, all lovers must
    Consign to thee, and come to dust.

No exorciser harm thee!
    Nor no witchcraft charm thee!
Ghost unlaid forbear thee!
    Nothing ill come near thee!

Quiet consummation have;
    And renowned be thy grave!

                          List then. Your cousin,
Mounted upon a steed that Emily
Did first bestow on him, a black one, owing
Not a hair-worth of white, which some will say
Weakens his price, and many will not buy
His goodness with this note—which superstition
Here finds allowance—on this horse is Arcite
Trotting the stones of Athens, which the calkins
Did rather tell than trample, for the horse
Would make his length a mile, if't pleased his rider
To put pride in him. As he thus went counting
The flinty pavement, dancing as 'twere to th' music
His own hoofs made—for as they say from iron
Came music's origin—what envious flint,
Cold as old Saturn, and like him possessed
With fire malevolent, darted a spark,
Or what fierce sulphur else to this end made,
I comment not: the hot horse, hot as fire,
Took toy at this, and fell to what disorder
His power could give his will, bounds, comes
    on end,
Forgets school-doing, being therein trained
And of kind manage; pig-like he whines
At the sharp rowel, which he frets at rather
Than any jot obeys; seeks all foul means

Of boist'rous and rough jadery to dis-seat
His lord, that kept it bravely. When nought served,
When neither curb would crack, girth break, nor
    diff'ring plunges
Dis-root his rider whence he grew, but that
He kept him 'tween his legs, on his hind hoofs
On end he stands,
That Arcite's legs being higher than his head
Seemed with strange art to hang; his victor's
    wreath
Even then fell off his head; and presently
Backward the jade comes o'er, and his full poise
Becomes the rider's load. Yet is he living,
But such a vessel 'tis that floats but for
The surge that next approaches.

                                     Safely in harbour
Is the king's ship; in the deep nook, where once
Thou call'dst me up at midnight to fetch dew
From the still-vex'd Bermoothes; there she's hid:
The mariners all under hatches stow'd;
Who, with a charm join'd to their suffer'd labour,
I have left asleep: and for the rest o' the fleet
Which I dispers'd, they all have met again,
And are upon the Mediterranean flote,
Bound sadly home for Naples,
Supposing that they saw the king's ship wrack'd,
And his great person perish.

I dream'd there was an Emperor Anthony:
O! such another sleep, that I might see
But such another man....
His face was as the heavens, and therein stuck
A sun and moon, which kept their course, and
    lighted
The little O, the earth....
His legs bestrid the ocean; his rear'd arm
Crested the world; his voice was propertied
As all the tuned spheres, and that to friends;
But when he meant to quail and shake the orb,
He was as rattling thunder. For his bounty,
There was no winter in't, an autumn 'twas
That grew the more by reaping; his delights
Were dolphin-like, they show'd his back above
The element they liv'd in; in his livery
Walk'd crowns and crownets, realms and islands
    were
As plates dropp'd from his pocket.

Where should this music be? i' th' air, or th' earth?
It sounds no more;—and sure, it waits upon
Some god o' th' island. Sitting on a bank,
Weeping again the king my father's wrack,
This music crept by me upon the waters,
Allaying both their fury, and my passion,
With its sweet air: thence I have follow'd it.—
Or it hath drawn me rather,—but 'tis gone.

No, it begins again.
Full fathom five thy father lies;
   Of his bones are coral made:
Those are pearls that were his eyes:
   Nothing of him that doth fade,
But doth suffer a sea-change
Into something rich and strange.
Sea-nymphs hourly ring his knell:
                     Ding-dong.
Hark! now I hear them,—ding-dong, bell.

                           With fairest flowers
While summer lasts and I live here, Fidele,
I'll sweeten thy sad grave; thou shalt not lack
The flower that's like thy face, pale primrose, nor
The azur'd hare-bell, like thy veins, no, nor
The leaf of eglantine, whom not to slander,
Out-sweeten'd not thy breath: the ruddock would,
With charitable bill,—O bill! sore-shaming
Those rich-left heirs, that let their fathers lie
Without a monument,—bring thee all this;
Yea, and furr'd moss besides, when flowers are none,
To winter-ground thy corse.

Ye elves of hills, brooks, standing lakes, and groves;
And ye, that on the sands with printless foot

Do chase the ebbing Neptune and do fly him
When he comes back; you demi-puppets, that
By moonshine do the green sour ringlets make
Whereof the ewe not bites; and you, whose pastime
Is to make midnight mushrooms; that rejoice
To hear the solemn curfew; by whose aid,—
Weak masters though ye be—I have bedimm'd
The noontide sun, call'd forth the mutinous winds,
And 'twixt the green sea and the azur'd vault
Set roaring war: to the dread-rattling thunder
Have I given fire and rifted Jove's stout oak
With his own bolt; the strong-bas'd promontory
Have I made shake; and by the spurs pluck'd up
The pine and cedar; graves at my command
Have wak'd their sleepers, op'd, and let them forth
By my so potent art. But this rough magic
I here abjure; and, when I have requir'd
Some heavenly music,—which even now I do,—
To work mine end upon their senses that
This airy charm is for, I'll break my staff,
Bury it certain fathoms in the earth,
And, deeper than did ever plummet sound,
I'll drown my book.

A terrible child-bed hast thou had, my dear;
No light, no fire: the unfriendly elements
Forgot thee utterly; nor have I time
To give thee hallow'd to thy grave, but straight

Must cast thee, scarcely coffin'd, in the ooze;
Where, for a monument upon thy bones,
And aye-remaining lamps, the belching whale
And humming water must o'erwhelm thy corpse,
Lying with simple shells!

Our revels now are ended. These our actors,
As I foretold you, were all spirits and
Are melted into air, into thin air:
And, like the baseless fabric of this vision,
The cloud-capp'd towers, the gorgeous palaces,
The solemn temples, the great globe itself,
Yea, all which it inherit, shall dissolve
And, like this insubstantial pageant faded,
Leave not a rack behind. We are such stuff
As dreams are made on, and our little life
Is rounded with a sleep.

Let the bird of loudest lay,
On the sole Arabian tree,
Herald sad and trumpet be,
To whose sound chaste wings obey.

But thou shrieking harbinger,
Foul precursor of the fiend,
Augur of the fever's end,
To this troop come thou not near.

From this session interdict
Every fowl of tyrant wing,
Save the eagle, feather'd king:
Keep the obsequy so strict.

Let the priest in surplice white
That defunctive music can,
Be the death-divining swan,
Lest the requiem lack his right.

And thou treble-dated crow,
That thy sable gender mak'st
With the breath thou giv'st and tak'st,
'Mongst our mourners shalt thou go.

Here the anthem doth commence:
Love and constancy is dead;
Phoenix and the turtle fled
In a mutual flame from hence.

So they lov'd, as love in twain
Had the essence but in one;
Two distincts, division none:
Number there in love was slain.

Hearts remote, yet not asunder;
Distance, and no space was seen
'Twixt the turtle and his queen:
But in them it were a wonder.

So between them love did shine,
That the turtle saw his right
Flaming in the phoenix' sight;
Either was the other's mine.

Property was thus appall'd,
That the self was not the same;
Single nature's double name
Neither two nor one was call'd.

Reason, in itself confounded,
Saw division grow together;
To themselves yet either neither,
Simple were so well compounded,

That it cried, "How true a twain
Seemeth this concordant one!
Love hath reason, reason none,
If what parts can so remain."

Whereupon it made this threne
To the phoenix and the dove,
Co-supremes and stars of love,
As chorus to their tragic scene.

Threnos

Beauty, truth, and rarity
Grace in all simplicity,
Here enclos'd in cinders lie.

Death is now the phoenix' nest;
And the turtle's loyal breast
To eternity doth rest,

Leaving no posterity:
'Twas not their infirmity,
It was married chastity.

Truth may seem, but cannot be;
Beauty brag, but 'tis not she;
Truth and beauty buried be.

To this urn let those repair
That are either true or fair;
For these dead birds sigh a prayer.

APPENDIX